THE YOGA OF CONSCIOUSNESS

THE YOGA OF CONSCIOUSNESS

25 Direct Practices to Enlightenment.

**Revealing the Missing Keys to Self-Realization.
Beyond Kundalini, Kriya Yoga & all Spirituality into
Awakening Non-Duality.**

- BOOK 4 -

SANTATAGAMANA

Copyright © 2018 by SantataGamana

All rights reserved.

1st Edition, May 2018

ISBN: 978-1719017954

No portion of this book may be reproduced in any form, including photocopying, recording, or any electronic or mechanical methods, without permission from the author except for brief quotes.

Special thanks to Eric Robins, who edited and proofread this book with profound love, kindness, and dedication.

Cover art: Titima Ongkantong/Shutterstock.com

Disclaimer for Legal Purposes

The information provided in this book is strictly for reference only and is not in any manner a substitute for medical advice. In the case of any doubt, please contact your healthcare provider. The author assumes no responsibility or liability for any injuries, negative consequences or losses that may result from practicing what is described in this book. Any perceived slights of specific people or organizations are unintentional. All the names referred to in this book are for illustrative purposes only, are the property of their respective owners and not affiliated with this publication in any way.

Read also, by the same author of *The Yoga of Consciousness*:

— KRIYA YOGA EXPOSED

The Truth About Current Kriya Yoga Gurus & Organizations.
Going Beyond Kriya, Contains the Explanation of a Special Technique
Never Revealed Before in Kriya Literature.

— THE SECRET POWER OF KRIYA YOGA

Revealing the Fastest Path to Enlightenment.
How Fusing Bhakti & Jnana Yoga into Kriya will Unleash the most
Powerful Yoga Ever.

— KUNDALINI EXPOSED

Disclosing the Cosmic Mystery of Kundalini.
The Ultimate Guide to Kundalini Yoga, Kundalini Awakening, Rising,
and Reposing on its Hidden Throne.

Available @ Amazon as Kindle & Paperback.

Subscribe and receive the ebook **Uncovering the Real**
plus updates and information regarding new books or
articles, which will be sent about once a month.
www.RealYoga.info

If you have any doubts or questions regarding this or any
of the other books, feel free to contact me at:
Santata@RealYoga.info

Some say that my teaching is nonsense.
Others call it lofty but impractical.
But to those who have looked inside themselves,
this nonsense makes perfect sense.
And to those who put it into practice,
this loftiness has roots that go deep.

- LAO TZU
TAO TE CHING

TABLE OF CONTENTS

Introduction   **13**

Part I – The False Self

  1. Hello Ego, My Old Friend   19

  2. Revealing The "I"   27

  3. The Appearance   35

  4. The Imaginary Chains   41

  5. The Pitfall of Emotions   47

  6. The Spiritual Ego   53

  7. Don't Be Tricked by The Magician   59

  8. Spirituality Can Be The Ego's Playground 67

  9. Remain Like The Buddha   75

Part II – The True Self

  10. Without Anything, I Still Am   81

  11. Don't Resist Life   89

  12. The Power of Conscious Witnessing   97

  13. Recognize The Background   105

14. Freedom is Not an Object of Meditation 111

15. Understanding The Foundation of Spiritual Practice 117

16. Practicing Non-Duality 127

Part III – Breaking Free

17. What About my Personal Life? 143

18. The World is Yours 147

19. Surrendering 153

20. You Have What It Takes 157

21. Nothing 163

22. The Heart of Consciousness 169

Glossary 177

INTRODUCTION

You have been searching for something beyond yourself, beyond the mundane life, beyond the plastic flowers of human existence.

Yet, every time you seem to be closing in on the Truth, something has gotten in the way. Maybe you didn't even notice it, or maybe you did but temporarily gave up, or perhaps you persisted to this very day.

What you are looking for was probably never taught to you by your teachers, parents, culture, books, society, or even your spiritual guru. Even when something truthful was said, those were mere words grabbing your attention, perhaps providing a glimpse into your own thoughtless and blissful Consciousness, but more often than not, they were just stories you heard.

Yet despite many meditations, spiritual practices, pilgrimages, mystical experiences, and so on, you see yourself sidetracking from your spiritual journey, over and over again. It is as if it were stronger than you.

Motivation can only sustain your quest for so long. The illusion of Maya seems to seduce you, ever more subtly, as you progress along your spiritual path—or shall I say—in your path toward yourself.

Daily life and society have pulled your attention onto other subjects, "genuinely important subjects," society says. Those side-tracks eventually turned into your main focus, and now you live a life where you have a good job, a solid house and a warm family. At night, you read a spiritual book that keeps your heart alive, and sustains the delusion that one day you will discover the everlasting bliss of enlightenment sang and poetized by Saints and Sages. Or maybe you don't have a good job, a solid house or a warm family. Either way, this *ping-pong* game has to end.

Investigating further, one realizes that it's not truly society's fault, or anyone else's fault for that matter, but one's own. But, it's not really oneself! Rather, it's a little false self, posing as the real Self.

Its name: Ego.

This is a book for those who wish to put an end to all misery and dissatisfaction once and for all.

This is a book for those who have struggled with their meditation and spiritual endeavors for a long time but have yet to put an end to their persistent self-centeredness.

This is a practical guide for those who wish to put an end to the misery-creator known as ego.

This is a practical guide for those who wish to find their eternal completeness. 25 Non-dual practices will be given that point directly toward your true nature, helping you to recognize the eternal Consciousness within, and abide there. Please, do not skip ahead to those practices—they need a mature mind. Read the whole book in order, chapter by chapter, because in the rest of the book lie the missing keys to make these non-dual practices work.

Hopefully, this is not just *another* spiritual text you are reading. Do not use it as an instrument to increase your intellectual capacity, to discuss philosophy, or even to create new beliefs. Enough of those long, dense and complex spiritual volumes that often, rather than clarifying things for seekers, make them even more confused.

This book will help you to shorten your spiritual path by awakening real discrimination between the real and unreal, the eternal and temporary; and by unlocking profound Insight into your true absolute blissful nature.

The content presented herein is beyond common meditation or intellectual insights. Rather, it points toward the Consciousness that is prior to thought, ego, mind, and intellect. It guides you toward abiding in your own bodiless empty Consciousness, which is already the ever-present Truth, but seems to be obscured by the ever-deceiving ego.

Yet, there's a high chance that the egoic mind will not readily accept this text. To combat that, I will be repeating the same instructions throughout the book in different ways.

Every practitioner will face countless obstacles. Although they are illusory, since their very source, the ego, is also illusory, they need to be dissolved with the light of Awareness.

You can practice right after reading this book. Or at least repose for 5 minutes, just being still. Let the energy fill you up, quieting or even stopping your mind temporarily. That's much more important than words. Even though they may seem like a big deal, because they help us to convey information, intellectual knowledge and instructions, words are actually the least important part of what I'm trying to communicate here. It is the direct experience from which everything arises that is the true pearl we're trying to reach in the deep ocean dive we call our spiritual journey.

By showing you how the ego works behind the scenes, and leads you to live a life of dissatisfaction and incompleteness, you will finally wake up to your true purpose of attaining Freedom. All ego mechanisms, schemes and deceiving tricks will be exposed.

This publication should be read with extreme awareness

and focus, as if you were meditating. It has the power to elevate your normal day-to-day consciousness to a higher meditative-consciousness. Please be open-minded and consider the chance that what will be revealed points toward the Truth that the ego often seemingly obstructs.

Most books or motivational talks and videos mention a "call for action." That has its place, for sure, but this book is different. When we are dealing with Freedom and enlightenment, then we have to take a different approach. Yes, we all start with action and with doing, but eventually have to revert to "non-doing."

This volume is a call for "inaction"—inaction of noise, mental noise. This doesn't mean a dull or lethargic mind, but a purely sharp mind. A mind using 100% of its power of attention, which is one of its greatest powers, to be mindfully aware. It is beyond all scriptural knowledge, all intellectual analysis, all meditation and all spiritual practices, where the effortlessness of "just Being" and abiding in the background of consciousness arises in oneself.

Most people have understood and can apply the energetic practices from whichever tradition they are following, but many seem to struggle with the "I am-ness," the "just Being," which can also be called *Parvastha* (in Kriya Yoga), "just sitting" (in Zen Buddhism) or the Presence of Being. This publication will guide you experientially to abiding in consciousness, effortlessly. It's not a mere philosophy—it's the bridge toward true and perpetual Freedom. This guide will make it accessible, direct, and practical.

For a long time you've been invested in your current way of living, afraid of climbing the ultimate step into the unknown, bound by the ego's illusions. As long as you keep investing in your current way of living, you will not climb the ultimate step into the unknown.

Recognizing the "I-ego," dissolving it and living without it, is truly being enlightened. This phantom self—created by the ignorance of our true nature, along with its weapons of personhood formed by the unconscious identification with the thinking and divisive mind—is finally running out of time.

Are you ready to dive into this unknown?

> "When nothing is done, nothing is left undone."
> — LAO TZU, TAO TE CHING

PART I – THE FALSE SELF

CHAPTER 1

HELLO EGO, MY OLD FRIEND

Humans are afraid of facing themselves. We live a particular kind of life, think in a certain way, have habits, patterns, beliefs, likes, dislikes, opinions, hopes, and so on, and we want none of that to be disturbed. We refuse to accept the unknowingness that comes when we get out of our "person-zone." Unknowingness seems to us as if it were death's sickle. It brings fear.

But it is this unknowingness that we must dive into. It is this unknowingness that we must have the courage to face. After all, we will face it on our deathbed, perhaps semi-consciously or even entirely unconscious. So why not face it right now with a lucid and clear awareness?

Let's start by investigating who we think we are.

When you were in school, you probably had to write an essay about yourself. You talked about when you were born, how old you were, who your parents were, what you liked to do in your free time, which cartoons you enjoyed watching, what you wanted to do when you grew up, which mental characteristics you possessed (e.g., "I am stubborn, but very smart."), and so on.

But is this really who you are? How you described yourself when you were eight years old is very different from how you would describe yourself at 15, which in turn would be completely different if you were to write it when you were 50 years old. Can you be this ever-changing *persona*?

Most people, when asked "Who are you?" will answer something like:

I am *[name]*, a *[job title]*. I am *[age]* years old, and I live in *[city/state/country]*. I was born in *[city/state/country]*, and I enjoy *[activity]* in my free time.

Don't be fooled. That is not who you are.

People who get involved with spirituality, who often think they are superior to "ignorant" or "unawakened" people also come up with similar answers.

I am *[initiation-given spiritual name]*, a follower of *[guru]*, from *[lineage name]*. I practice *[tradition name]*, which is the best spiritual tradition/practice in the world. The *[some Divine being name]* blesses my practice and life.

Not that there's anything wrong with that, but such behavior exhibits a strong ego and a fierce focus on "me" and "mine," exposing a blind attachment to whatever tradition or spiritual practice they follow.

This is all *ego-talk*. Even most *spiritual-talk* is *ego-talk*. I will go one step further and say that frequently, spiritual books are full of self-centered talk. It's as if the world spins around the author, his or her tradition, and methodology. It's rare to find one who doesn't belong to such a group. You need a high discernment and sensitivity to feel one who's talking from pure Consciousness, from the true Heart, rather than from the ego, the false self.

The false self, "I-ego," is an old friend, but such friendship has become impossible to sustain. It's time to say goodbye.

When you were born, you were not aware of your "self." You were aware in the sense of being aware by simply being, but not in the sense of "I am so-and-so." You were unselfconscious. With time, and due to the imposed otherness, together with the external expansion of the senses, the consciousness contracted and started identifying with the body more and more. There was no conditioned mind yet, but this sense of "I," which has its basis on "I am the body," steadily gained momentum and came into full being.

Every being that comes into this world has to experience this "I" and "other." Even every enlightened being had to pass through such an experience, which is the root trauma—the sense of a separate self. This is an apparent traumatic contraction in the boundless Consciousness. The more we derive our sense of self from this contraction, the "I-ego," and the more we believe in its thoughts, the more are we bound to suffer.

In fact, the ego controls all thoughts, and it will not let itself be exposed for what it is. It will always interpret what is being written in a way that aligns best with its egoic self-interest, directing your attention and motivation in such a manner that it preserves itself. It often operates stealthily, never allowing you to see how you are projecting your own insecurities and flaws onto someone else or some situation.

For example, people often see things in books that aren't even there. When the ego feels threatened by a teaching, it will distort it, misinterpreting to the point of imagining problems and things that are not actually in that teaching.

I am saying this early on so that you do not let it get in the way when reading this volume. Stay lucid and read with the deepest possible awareness. The ego cannot understand this book—only you can.

Most aspirants lack the needed discernment to realize that. Even these words you're reading right now might be enough to make the ego go on a rampage, or elicit a feeling of denial.

If you are not interested in Self-Realization, Freedom, Truth, peace, bliss, wisdom, unimaginable happiness and completeness beyond all understanding, you can stop reading now.

On the other hand, if you are genuine and honest with yourself, I suggest you really start paying attention to your thoughts and reactions when reading this book. Do not allow the ego to distort what is being shared here. Do not let the ego take the teachings herein and change them into a means of self-preservation.

Dissolving the "I-ego" is the toughest adventure a human being can pursue because it involves giving up everything, letting go of not only the personality but all of its adjuncts— memories, dreams, goals, personal story, etc. It's not that one can't be successful regarding *society-mayic-existence*, finances or academic prestige. All of these things can be accomplished, but not as an "I" accomplishing them. While the sense of doership[1] is active, one is bound by the ego chains, always feeling incomplete and ultimately unfulfilled.

The ego has a deep-rooted sense of lack, of not being complete. This translates into a search for "something," whatever it is—money, fame, success, adventure, loving relationships,

---

[1] Acting without the sense of being the doer. Refer to *Kundalini Exposed*, chapter 4, *The Importance of Kundalini Awakening*.

THE YOGA OF CONSCIOUSNESS

the "perfect" physical appearance, etc. It's a never-ending wanting and needing. It can either be a conscious knowing of incompleteness, or unconscious.

When the ego is running your life, this "always-desiring-something-and-never-at-peace" feeling will never end. *Never.* Some people will even experience it on their death-bed, for example lamenting that they could've done something different, or trying to make peace with people they've had disputes with.

Besides for the brief happiness you feel after having accomplished whatever you desired, you will never truly be at ease, peaceful or happy, for desires always carry the seed of discontentment. The ego will always want something more. *Always.*

This is often seen as a good thing in society, "Never let your fire die. Always go further and deeper into your dreams! Always go for more, never stop!"

I know I'll be misunderstood by what is written above, and many people will disagree with it. But bear with me:

Always wanting more and more shows how dissatisfied and incomplete one really is. Such a person is never at peace, never permanently fulfilled or happy, never stress-free. The only reason you dream of achieving something is because you can't see that you're already the Whole. True everlasting tranquility seems impossible.

Realize that your dreams have also been written by the ego. This is a tough teaching, and very few aspirants will grasp what is being conveyed. It doesn't mean you can't or shouldn't follow your dreams, but it does mean that you should investigate whose dreams they are, when and why they arose, what their ultimate purpose is, what they will bring you, and so on. Go really deep with these questions—do not stay just at the surface.

Now, on the other hand, I can tell you that whatever you wish to do while still bound by the "I-ego" will never be as good as if it were done without an ego. Where do you think all those moments of inspiration or "eureka" come from? Not from the ego. The purest moments, when one is truly present, are spontaneous and impersonal. When a performer, whomever he or she is, is doing his or her performance, being dance, music, sports, or whatever it is, if they are truly in the present moment, fully giving their all, spontaneously, the ego's grip over them is temporarily lessened. It is beautiful.

When a scientist makes an amazing discovery, that discovery comes from a "person-less place." It never comes from the ego! Whenever one is "in the zone," totally immersed in whatever one is doing, it's an absorption, similar to a semi-meditative state. Not only does one seem to lose the sense of time and space, but the "I am a person" and all of its baggage is temporarily forgotten!

What's better to achieve your dreams than being egoless? Everything is so much better without an ego.

I just can't promise that you will still want to achieve those myriad things when you dissolve your ego, especially when you realize the emptiness of everything-ness. But that's another story, one that will happen when there's no longer a narrator.

CHAPTER 2

REVEALING THE "I"

Ego is "I," the thought "I." Before anything can be, such as "I am a man" or "I am a woman," "I" has to be there. "I" is, therefore, the foundation of duality. All duality stands on "I." Without "I," there can never be a "you," an "other," or anything else.

There are different types of definitions of what ego means, but in this book, ego means the thought "I," which is based on the belief "I am the body." All conditionings, which pertain to the psychological mind[2] are based on the notion of "I," or "I am the body." They are like tomato sauce's stains in one's clothing. We can wash and remove those stains, but it's not easy, and there's no guarantee we won't get our clothes dirty again. Wasting lifetimes progressively removing these conditionings will not cut it, especially since new ones might appear.

---

[2] The part of the mind that creates your story and interprets it, identifying with thought and its projections, inevitably causing suffering.

Consciousness, by identifying with a body ("I am the body"), assumes a name, a story, a complex mixture of ideas, beliefs, opinions, memories, and then holding it all together creates a personality out of it—"I am Mark," for example.

The ego can have millions of adjuncts, like the abovementioned. Changing all of those adjuncts (e.g., an aggressive person undergoes therapy and comes out calm and kind), does not change the ego ("I"). It only changes its adjuncts. An "I" is always an "I" unless it is dissolved (enlightenment).

Robert was born a male: "I am Robert" - "I am a man."

When he was 21 years old, he made male-to-female gender reassignment surgery, becoming "Jessie," a woman: "I am Jessie" - "I am a woman."

Did the "I" change?

No. The underlying principle of being an individual self remained, even though two core adjuncts changed—the name and gender.

This clearly shows that no matter how much we evolve, how much self-development we do, how much we improve our personality, our business and social skills, how many languages we speak or different kinds of meditation we know and do, all changes pertain to the ego, and the ego only. Yet the ego itself doesn't change—its foundation, the "I am the body" belief, remains the same. Only direct realization of our real bodiless nature can truly dissolve that primal ignorance (intellectually knowing that you're not the body is not enough).

It is all these adjuncts that give this false sense of self the feeling of being real. It is not real, but it has powerful building blocks that make it seem real.

How then can we realize our "I-less" nature, our inherent interconnectedness?

A fail-proof method is to dissolve the root of those conditionings, the "I-ego," precisely as will be explained in this book.

Without "I," without the sense of being a separate self, there is no conditioning. It's because of this root, the ego, that all suffering, dissatisfaction, misery, and unhappiness can germinate. Their opposites also feed off the ego, but a dualistic joy, a brief satisfaction, or a short burst of happiness are always surrounded by their opposites and not considered worth pursuing. In duality, every pleasure contains within itself the seed of pain, its inseparable opposite which will manifest in time. Satisfaction in duality is only an interval between various dissatisfactions. Only the happiness of Being is everlasting and not subject to fluctuations due to

THE YOGA OF CONSCIOUSNESS

external events. This happiness is the natural fragrance of an egoless consciousness.

However, some degree of mind purification is needed at the beginning, because a less conditioned mind not only brings more peace and joy to our life, but is the basis that allows us to truly shed some blazing light on the phantom ego, unveiling its non-existent nature[3]. Nevertheless, it's worth emphasizing that continuously cleaning the dust off the screen (of consciousness) will be a lifetime(s) duty. That's what the ego wants!

Furthermore, it believes itself to be a real self; it really believes its personality is something tangible, something of value. It actually thinks it is some sort of entity. That's why it is afraid of ending. It thinks it's going to die, and fears non-existence. But how can a mirage die? It can only be realized that it's an illusion. It is neither a "thing," nor does it live "inside you." It's a false sense of self, leading you to conclude that you are separate from the rest of the world.

It is the source of all problems and suffering. This sense of separateness creates a multitude of belief systems, dogmas, superiority and inferiority complexes, hate, dissatisfaction,

---

[3] Reading this book also purifies your mind. Whenever you come in contact with genuine words and energy, if you allow them to go deep within your being, your mind will shed a lot of conditionings, from beliefs to blockages, allowing a higher wisdom and awareness to arise.

misery, etc. Name anything negative in this world, and you can always trace it back to the ego and its preposterous interpretations and thoughts. Not that it is "evil" or anything like that, but this is just its nature, in the same way that a lion isn't evil for killing a gazelle. The ego serves the purpose of experiencing duality, a separate existence. The problem is that it brings suffering and incompleteness with it. It is temporary, limited and ever-lacking. It is the moving film in the eternal, unchanging screen of unlimited Consciousness.

Additionally, being temporary, it can never be of value. It appears posing as us after what some call "enlightenment experience," such as formless absorption (*Asamprajnata/ Nirvikalpa Samadhi* or the "experience" of *emptiness* or *nothingness*), or the so-called unconscious state, like deep dreamless sleep and general anesthesia. When it arises, "we" awaken either in the dream state or the waking state. Even any "life" in other dimensions, worlds, realities, astral realms, sub or supra worlds, "afterlife"—you name it—it's still the ego ("I"). It doesn't matter how subtle it gets; if there is a sense of "self," a separation, duality, then it's an egoic state.

Since it's not permanent, it's not worth much. Sooner or later—when the body dies, when the energetic, pranic, astral, mental, subtle, causal, or any other body that one can think

THE YOGA OF CONSCIOUSNESS

of dissolves, the ego will end. There's no such thing as an immortal body, immortal "I," or immortal entity. Even if just at the end of this universal cycle when the Universe dissolves back to its original singularity—everything that had a beginning will end.

Yet, there is eternal life in you. You are eternal life. Your true Self, the pure empty space of Awareness where the ego-self seems to appear and disappear, is eternal and not subject to any change or lack. The realization of being unborn, deathless and limitless is worth pursuing.[4]

All humans, unless they have liberated themselves, are puppets to the ego. The false self controls all thoughts, emotions, opinions, beliefs, interpretations, concepts, ideas, expectations, actions, and reactions. Unless one is absolutely empty, and allows life to naturally flow through, spontaneously living as one with the whole, the ego will always be in control. Committing suicide or harming the body serves no purpose whatsoever. Physical death does not end the ego; it will just form a new body and keep dreaming. Those are not ways to end the ego's monarchy.

Thinking that you've come up to an impossible-to-overcome stumbling block is merely another thought also—it is

---

[4] Refer to *The Secret Power of Kriya Yoga*, chapter 19, *The Absolute Beyond Comprehension;* and *Kundalini Exposed*, chapter 3, *Consciousness*.

not true. It doesn't matter if you've never meditated before, or if you've been into spirituality for 50 years, 500 lifetimes, or it's the first time you're reading about the truth—no matter where you are, how old you are, whether you're male or female, what your past has been, how unfit, ignorant or smart you think you are, how your current life situation is, if you are sick, depressed, hurt, sad, miserable, rich, poor, etc.—everything's possible. *Everything is possible.* Never give up and never believe what your ego or others tell you. Go for your own direct realization of God, of the Truth, of already being what you are attempting to be—Unbroken Wholeness.

Screen of Consciousness

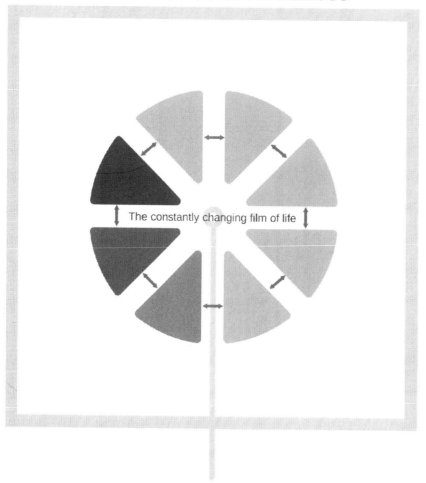

The constant flux of the mind creates the illusion of a self, which is also a phenomenon on the screen of consciousness. Consciousness believes it is an ever-changing & perishable object ("I am so-and-so").

CHAPTER 3

THE APPEARANCE

Before the ego came into being, there was no body, no mind, no name, no parents, no age, no problems, no desires, no needs, no concepts, no ideas, no beliefs, no words, no knowledge, no meditation, no spirituality, no ignorance, no Liberation, and no enlightenment.

The ego has desires only if something is absent. You desire this thing, that thing, and so on. When the ego came, everything came with it. Whenever we are free from the egoistic notion of being an individual entity, we are happy. Whenever we are bound to the conviction of being an individual entity, we are unhappy. This individuation promotes cravings and desires; without it, they all dissipate. The seeming appearance of this "I" can be called the spontaneous dual existence of the ineffable non-dual Absolute, which is pure Consciousness alone, without any content, any illusion or any identification. That is your true and perfect home. It is completeness.

It is through duality, through the experience of a separate self that the Unknowable can know itself. It is as if the Unknown came into duality and came to be known (in its manifested aspect). Eventually, it will be absorbed back into the Unknown. The limitless can't know that it is limitless[5] unless it tastes limits before coming back in awe to its limitlessness.

Consciousness initially emerges in the body[6] as a "pure mind," being impersonal, as a newborn baby. It doesn't differentiate or think. It just is. A newborn baby is merely aware—not lost in thought believing itself to be some personality nor dwelling on a past history related drama.

Some subtle desires and traumas might have come from previous lives though, buried deep in the unconscious in "seed form," because when the body dies, the ego stays alive but dreams a new body and personality, "saving" only the deepest "root" aspects. As an easier to understand example, one could say it is similar to a dream, where although the "dream-you" is different than the "you" of your current life, some desires, traumas, problems or certain traits have

---

[5] It's not that it "can't" because it is limited or something like that, but because there's no need for it to. Both "limitless" and "limits" are concepts within duality.

[6] This consciousness is but a reflection of pure Consciousness. Both the body and the "pure mind" are but a motion picture on the screen of consciousness.

projected onto it, and you, in that dream-body, are experiencing these and living that dream-life.

This means that life after life, the more desires and beliefs you accumulate, the more they have a chance of storing up on the unconscious mind (as if they were "occult files"). These subsequently need to be brought up to the conscious mind to be purified or cleaned through spiritual practice.

Body-consciousness is entirely related to world-consciousness. When there is body-consciousness (ego), there is consciousness of the world (the diverse universe of names and forms). When there is no body-consciousness, there is no world-consciousness. Even if someone were to say that "When I die, I become a spirit, and can still astral travel to this world," that would not refute the abovementioned. Even supposing that someone becomes an "astral spirit" and can still "travel to this world," they would still have an ego and subtle body-consciousness, hence still perceiving and being aware of the world.

Often people ask whether there are other dimensions and levels of dual existence, since at least half of spiritual literature is about that. Yes, there are, but they are not the Ultimate Reality; they are merely subtle forms of mayic existence, still bound to suffering or incompleteness. It doesn't matter how pure and heavenly some other realm is, eventually it will end.

Creation is cyclic—in the end it will all get dissolved back to the singularity, just to be recreated again. This makes Time the master of all worlds, universes, dimensions, realms, on all planes—physical, astral, mental, etc. All of these are still an ego perceiving something, through either the gross or subtle senses.

Pure Consciousness is beyond time—hence it doesn't decay or dissolve. It wasn't even born, so it can't die. It is not in space-time, but beyond. It's the substratum that allows all of those realms to even exist, just like H_2O is the basis of water, ice, and vapor.

Our true highest state is not even a state, and is beyond the mind, beyond the senses, beyond everything. The "closest" a normal human being gets to it is during unconsciousness or deep sleep. But as the identification with the mind is so strong, when humans wake up, all they know is "there was a blank, a nothingness, an emptiness..." The mind can't translate what is beyond it.

Your spiritual journey might take you to those realms, you might interact with other beings and so on, but this secret is essential to know: *Don't get caught up in it.*

Too many people get caught up in those realms, which can be extremely pleasant, beautiful, blissful, mysterious, adventurous, and so on—and not go all the way to the "end." With an incomplete journey, they will then have to reincarnate to go deeper (not necessarily in the physical realm). Ultimately, it can be a big detour, although a pleasing one.

CHAPTER **4**

THE IMAGINARY CHAINS

The majority of humanity lives in a delusion. Imagining that a thought ("I") is who you really are is the biggest delusion ever. All other delusions are built upon this primal ignorance. It's time to stop tolerating the one that has caused you so much suffering.

Understand that even something as ordinary as an itch on your arm during spiritual practice can bring suffering and desire. As you know, you should keep the body still during meditation. However, suppose an irritating itch appears— what do you do? You simply ignore it.

As you continue ignoring it, it grows stronger and starts burning. Now you're suffering, and you *really want* to scratch the arm to alleviate the discomfort. This situation makes such a desire not only pop up in the center of your mind, but also grabs your attention even more intensely. Yet the "meditation manual" says not to move, and to ignore

THE YOGA OF CONSCIOUSNESS

itches, making you not want to move either, because you're afraid it might disrupt your practice.

How to solve such a dilemma? You will keep suffering if you don't eliminate the itch, and you will suffer if you eliminate it. Aversion, desire, suffering, everything is there, in a simple itch. What a mess. This is an excellent metaphor for common life. Welcome to an ego-based life.

In such a life, humans always have their attention turned toward 3rd person objects[7], whether the objects are physical or non-physical, like thoughts. They never pay attention to that which is paying attention to something. Whenever attention is taken away from objects and put back on itself, it will start dissolving the knot of ignorance[8]. Usually, this is hard to do because our mental tendencies and habits make objectless awareness or the state of empty consciousness challenging to abide in and sustain. Paying attention to an object is so much easier than paying attention to no object at all!

That's why aspirants generally start by practicing easier forms of meditation like breath-awareness, or even grosser forms of spirituality like dualistic bhakti rituals. All of these

---

[7] In this book, whatever you can perceive is considered an object.

[8] The knot that binds consciousness to the latent tendencies and subtle desires, which is only cut when you "attain" enlightenment. Refer to the chapter "Spiritual Practice Process" in *Kriya Yoga Exposed*.

have the purpose of calming the mind and of purifying it so that it can sustain prolonged attention on an objectless awareness.

This objectless awareness is precisely what Kriya Yoga's after-state called *Parvastha* is, what abiding in "I am," "staying Present," "just Being," "falling back into the background witness," or Self-Awareness are. That's the state we have to be in.

The limited and distorted consciousness that we call ego sustains its seeming reality by attending to everything besides itself. In states such as deep dreamless sleep, our individual self subsides, but it will eventually rise and flourish once again as soon as we start dreaming or wake up, both of which are just states based on thinking.

To keep up the illusion, the ego always needs to identify with external things (thoughts included). These are the food with which it is constantly fed. By grasping an illusory body as itself, and by continually attending to objects, it gains strength and flourishes. On the other hand, if we investigate closely, attending to no objects whatsoever, it disappears. When the ego-consciousness turns within and breaks the chains binding it to its illusory body, it just vanishes. In the absence of a limited consciousness, the non-limited consciousness spontaneously shines.

Some more prominent objects of identification that the ego grasps are your personal story (which includes beliefs, views, acquired knowledge, etc.), job, social status, fame, possessions, relationships, and all kinds of individual (e.g., "I am a misunderstood genius,") and collective identifications (e.g., "I am vegan").

Your identity is none of these, and this is not a belief. Can you find yourself in any of those things? Certainly not. You must realize, by yourself, who or what your true Self really is. If any of those were you, if even your body or your personality were you, you would bring them with you after dying. Furthermore, they would be present whenever you were unconscious. But they aren't.

You are and exist whenever your physical body is present, but, for you, during a dream, that body is not present, but you still are and exist. This means that you are and exist whenever you live from your physical body, but you still are and exist whenever you are in a dream and living from that dream body, without the physical body being present. If the physical body were who you are, then it would always need to be present whenever you were. Whenever you were aware, the physical body would also have to be present. Since it is absent when you are dreaming, then it cannot be who you are.

You are and exist both whenever you are in the physical body or in a dream body. The body, personality or conditioning of each might be similar or different, but you, the substratum of both, are the same and continuous.

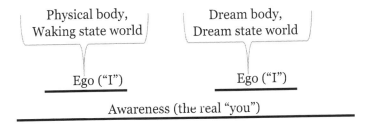

Did this sound confusing?

If the physical body were who you are, whenever you are aware, it would need to be present within your awareness. Otherwise, it's just an adjunct.

Are there any moments where you are not aware of your physical body? Yes, for example, whenever you are dreaming, you are still aware (aware of the dream-body and dream-world), but unaware of your physical body. That means the physical body cannot be who you are. You are beyond and free from its constraints. During unconsciousness, no body is present. Yet, you are still aware, of "nothingness." This Awareness, which is who you really are, is free from any adjuncts. Although you might have yet to realize it, you are already free—if you just drop the *imaginary* chain of identity.

CHAPTER 5

THE PITFALL OF EMOTIONS

All thoughts are opposed to your real immortal nature. Living life through the mind rather than through blissful consciousness is the root of all problems. After all, they can all be traced back to the ego.

Since for any thought to occur, there must first be an "I," then the mind's essence can be seen to be the thought "I" only. This thought "I" is just consciousness, but because it is aware of "otherness" and "other thoughts," and since it rises and falls after and before unconsciousness, it is not our true primal consciousness. It can only rise by identifying a physical body as "I," being a mixed form of consciousness and unconscious matter. It believes itself to be a body, giving rise to the "I am the body" idea, the "sin" talked about in Christianity.

When you say "I am such and such person," you are affirming that you are an independent consciousness that identifies itself with a specific body. This defines that consciousness as a person. Since that consciousness believes itself to be a specific body, it imprisons itself within the boundaries of that body, feeling separated from everything it perceives externally.

Our feeling of "I," which is attributed to the body and translates into "I am the body," is not real. You can easily realize this by seeing that the body is not aware of its own seeming existence—it has no awareness of its own.

It's important to clearly discern everything that you are not. The person you take yourself to be is perceived by you. Knowing this distinction is of utter importance. Whatever you can say about yourself is perceivable and subject to change, meaning it cannot be you. Identifying with what is "not you" will necessarily lead you to defend it—because someone or something can put it at risk, and you can lose it.

Emotions, for example, are just reactions to thoughts. If someone says something that offends you, your ego will start building up anger and rage toward that person. When the ego feels threatened, the body gets tight, breathing gets shallower and faster, and heat starts to build up as if you were about to fight for your life.

It doesn't even have to be an offensive statement that someone made to you; it can be as simple as someone challenging your beliefs or questioning your ability to do something.

The ego is a survival machine, concerned not only with body-survival but also with self-image survival. It tries, at all costs, to preserve the mental image it has of itself. That's why it is so hard to break someone's beliefs. The ego equates its life to deep-rooted beliefs, and since all beliefs are an illusion and are merely thoughts without any real direct experience basis, they are big obstacles to the realization of the Truth. For the ego, letting go of one of those core beliefs is dying.

A buildup of negative emotions or negative thoughts over time will undoubtedly lead to problems which could include anxiety, depression, fear, or even physical disease. By vibrationally living in such low frequency, you will start connecting more and more with that energy, even to the point of attracting events based on that energy.

Often, people are unaware of their own current state of being. They base who they are on the by-product of the identification of consciousness with the constant movement of the mind. They can become hypnotized and even lose lucidity to the point of having out-of-character unconscious reactions that don't match their personality (but were latently present all along).

Here's an example:

Martha, a 29-year-old woman who works in elder care services, was often verbally abused by the male patients she took care of. They insulted her, and let her know they didn't need or want her help. She was the single mom and provider for a 5-year-old, so quitting her job was out of the question. As the months passed by, she started accumulating a lot of frustration and anger toward those people she took care of. Martha never expressed it, but it was building up inside her, slowly making her life crumble. She would arrive home extremely tired and had little patience for her son. Martha used to be very kind and lovely, and she still is, but the situation at work was driving her crazy. One time, her son was playing in the living room and threw a ball toward the TV, causing it to fall from the TV stand and smash on the floor. She got furious and slapped him, and he started crying heavily since she had never hit him before.

Instantly, she regretted what she had done. All of that anger that had built up over the prior months finally came forward. Was Martha an angry person? No. But she took so much abuse and accumulated all that resentment to the point that she eventually exploded with her son.

A strong emotional pattern that keeps happening over and over again will ultimately manifest in a strong reaction. It doesn't matter if was initiated by others, by an external event, or even by ourselves.

That's why it's important to take things lightly. Never take anything personally, although it is understandable that a situation such as the one given above may be difficult to overcome. In that example, the elderly patients were just projecting their own resentment, anger, and frustration toward Martha. It was not her fault, and she certainly didn't do anything wrong.

Whenever one is not lucid enough, it is quite easy for a negative emotion to overpower one's state of mind, inevitably leading to non-conscious identification with it.

The ego can even grab positive attributes such as humility and compassion[9], attempting to appear humble and as a saint, but it's still camouflaged, feeding off such characteristics. Although externally it might look as if it were true humility, below the surface, the ego might be "Oh, look at how humble and spiritual I am."

Never try to be humble (or any other positive quality) in a "forcing" manner, because humility and modesty are directly related to the degree of strength the ego has over you. The less grip that the false-self has on you, the more kind and

---

[9] "I am enlightened."—the ego can even grab on to such statements, deluding itself into believing it has become enlightened.

THE YOGA OF CONSCIOUSNESS

humble you will be. If there is no ego, there is genuine humility and kindness. Please realize that your concept of what humility or kindness is might not be what true kindness or humility actually are. A true Guru yelling at a student might be a disguised sign of love and affection, for true kindness is helping the student to dissolve the ego.

Don't even listen to the solutions that the ego may try to present you with—they will never succeed because the ego itself is part of the problem. To be free from the turmoil of emotions that it causes, you have to refrain from deriving your sense of self from the phantom ego. Asking the ego to overcome the ego and all its suffering and incompleteness is like installing an antivirus to fix an infected computer when the antivirus is a virus itself!

Instead of looking for help in the mind, we go deeper. Of course we use the mind, initially, to try to sustain an empty Self-Awareness. Since the attention is not used to being "objectless," it will always try to catch some object to hold on to. Yet, with enough practice and dedication, the mind will start to abide more and more in emptiness, although there's still an effort, and thus a slight mental movement. However, as soon as we can abide "there" effortlessly, we are no longer using the mind. It has stopped its movements. Then, we are in no-mind. Being in no-mind over and over again is what finally "breaks" down the ego.

CHAPTER 6

THE SPIRITUAL EGO

As body-minds, our current behaviors and emotional reactions are shaped and influenced by our past experiences, often in an unconscious, automatic way. Once in a while, we are required to be consciously present to make an important decision, but mostly our lives seem to be lived by our conditioning on autopilot.

Our deeply rooted, programmed patterns of reaction are merely waiting for a particular kind of event to spur them to come to the surface. Some emotionally triggered situations seem to capture our attention so deeply that we appear to temporarily lose awareness of what's going on, reverting to unconscious conditioning mainly shaped in our childhood.

Starting from a very early age, the ego begins to accumulate traumas, insecurities, flaws, vulnerabilities, and so on. It doesn't require a complex situation or event either. Even something as basic as a young child running away from his mother in the supermarket, showing that he wants to be independent, will get the mother angry and scared. The child will then associate his independence from the mother with punishment. This can create massive insecurities in the toddler, making him susceptible to fear and anxiety, creating a very dependent personality.

On the other hand, if a mother allows her young child to run away from her (while she's secretly watching from afar), after a while the child will feel scared and alone, recognizing how powerless he is on his own. From this moment on, he might fear being separated from his mother, imprinting a tremendous sense of dependency on his mind. He may even feel guilty for running away from her.

The typical development of children will almost inevitably lead to adults with fragile personalities. Most of the time, even those adults who seem to exhibit tremendous confidence or "strong personalities" are just using masks superimposed on their fragile selves, either consciously or unconsciously, to avoid their deeper pain.

Insecurities and traumas don't happen exclusively during childhood either; they can happen during adulthood as well.

Many astute adults start reading self-help and personal development books and frequent similar websites in order to develop and further enhance their self (personality), but there undoubtedly comes a point when many turn to meditation, especially these days since it is very mainstream.

Yet their meditations only strengthen their sense of self, because they use them as a way to further enhance their egoic way of living, like improving cognitive ability to be better at work[10] or developing suprasensorial skills, rather than for awakening Insight and Liberation.

Eventually there comes a time, in this lifetime or another, when the very own ego realizes its utter powerlessness, completely surrendering to a "higher power." This realization of just how helpless the ego is to find everlasting happiness and peace, ends the ego's attempts to find completeness in the world, and gives birth to a true seeker of the Truth.

This seeker now starts reading deeper spiritual books and begins searching for a teacher or a guru, someone who can teach the path to enlightenment.

Being initiated into a tradition or a lineage of Masters can bring either profound humility and a feeling of being blessed, or profound arrogance and a feeling of superiority.

---

[10] Not that there is anything wrong with that. On the contrary, if everyone meditated to improve their mental abilities related to their work, jobs would be way better performed. With that said, the difference between meditating with the purpose of achieving Liberation, compared to training mind abilities is night and day.

THE YOGA OF CONSCIOUSNESS

Practicing some secret methodology to achieve "union with God" or to attain "enlightenment" creates a new sense of duty and responsibility in the seeker, reinforcing the need to achieve something that is currently missing. Now, practicing diligently every day, bowing to some deity or master in a frame, attending *satsangs* and retreats, and reading more and more spiritual books, are all part of the seeker's life.

Many years pass, and although the sincere seeker has become better at meditation, being capable of having stable attention for a longer period, having experienced some altered states of consciousness, some blissful, some not, having gained some minor insights into the nature of the world, being more devoted to the guru or lineage, having read hundreds of spiritual books and eating a plant-based diet, something is still missing.

It seems like although spirituality has brought a new sense of freshness and reality to the life of the seeker, a new spiritual identity was also born it with. The old identity, though some deep-rooted patterns still flare up once in a while, is no longer superficially present. A spiritual ego has been born, and this one is much subtler and smarter than the common or even intellectual ego.

This transition is inevitable. It doesn't have to be exactly like the aforementioned, but once a person goes from a "typical life" to a "spiritual life," the typical ego becomes a spiritual ego. It is expected, and one must be extremely alert when it happens. Why? Because this ego, knowing that something beyond itself is being pursued, will do all it can to prevent you from transcending it.

The human spiritual ego's tricks must now be exposed.

CHAPTER 7

DON'T BE TRICKED BY THE MAGICIAN

Thinking has become compulsive, getting out of hand. Usually, most of it is not only repetitive and useless, but also negative and damaging. It can lead to depression, and in some serious cases, to suicide.

The main issue is that compulsive thinking often goes unnoticed by most people since it has become a norm in their lives. How can someone live a genuinely peaceful and happy life when they are always constrained by the ego's chains?

Stress, anger, depression, and many other types of dysfunctional behaviors are frequently caused by obsessive thinking. It drains all the energy, making one mentally and physically tired, and never truly at ease.

The ego can be extremely dangerous because it has absolute control over your thoughts and actions, and yet flies unnoticed under the radar.

Thinking that if the mind or thinking stops equals the end of "me" is a severe delusion. You don't need to be in a vegetative state to have no thoughts; thinking is just one small feature of Consciousness. It cannot exist without Consciousness, but Consciousness exists without needing any thought. It is supposed to be a tool, not the master.

Thoughts control the "person," and since thoughts are controlled by the ego, the ego controls the person. At the end of the day, the ego itself is also a thought, but it is the primal thought which gives birth to all the other thoughts. However, the other thoughts are what give this primal thought a sense of existence. How paradoxically crazy is that?

Additionally, it has a multitude of tricks to prevent you from seeing the Truth within yourself. For example, have you ever noticed that the ego can convince you of anything?

Did you ever have one of those debates in school where a teacher says:

"Now you're against euthanasia – make an argument against it;"

And you do! You can find plenty of arguments against euthanasia.

Then, the teacher says, "Okay, now make an argument in its

favor!" And guess what? You do! You can, yet again, find plenty of arguments, but this time, in favor of euthanasia.

What does this show you? That the ego can find arguments in favor of anything, depending on your motivations. Yes, the ego doesn't care about the truth. It cares about being right and defending its position. Therefore, the ego finds arguments to either defend or attack based on the motivation, not on facts or the truth. And what does the ego really want, when you're looking to go beyond it? To preserve itself, to stay "alive."

Do you understand the consequences of what this means?

It means the ego will be able to find arguments for everything; it will be able to come up with an absolutely reasonable and logic explanation for *anything* so that it can survive and preserve itself.

Have you noticed this? No? That means the ego is tricking you, and you must start being lucidly aware. Enough sleeping, it's time to be present and conscious of how the ego is running your life!

Concepts, ideas, beliefs, basically anything that has its basis in thought must be discarded. It doesn't matter how subtle or spiritual it is, for it will keep feeding the ego. Having a spiritual ego is not better than having a "normal ego." It can be even worse since it's way subtler and harder to "catch."

This means one must be extremely careful not to get lost in a labyrinth of concepts and intellectual or scriptural knowledge. Direct experience awakens profound and real Insight, culminating in Liberation. That's the only thing that matters in spirituality.

Talking about climbing Mount Everest, creating mountain-climber groups or sites on the internet, attending lectures on climbing Everest or even reading books about mountain climbing and the Himalayan mountains will not give you the direct experience of actually climbing Mount Everest! You must climb Mount Everest to know exactly how climbing Mount Everest is! In the same way, you must climb out of the ego's dimension by abiding in empty Consciousness beyond any delusions.

Before reading this book, you probably were not aware of how the ego works to keep you imprisoned in thought. Being unconscious regarding the ego's stratagems means you are being manipulated by it and getting entangled even more in the dream. This is especially true because the ego can even hide its own schemes from itself.

Most spiritual teachings teach some form of meditation, such as breath-witnessing, pranayama, mantra, etc., from the very beginning. What they usually don't teach from the beginning is that you have to stay lucid and aware throughout the day, observing how the ego is controlling your reactions, thoughts, emotions, and actions. Cultivating this witnessing day-to-day is essential to awaken non-attachment, not just to the world and its shiny and fancy objects, but also to your own personality, habits, and patterns of emotional thought-reactions.

Another critical aspect of a real spiritual path that is seldom mentioned is self-honesty. Please, be honest with yourself. Even though admitting mistakes or errors might be tough (for the ego), it might be the first step in purifying your mind.

Do not keep supporting beliefs by affirming things you do not know either. There's no shame in saying "I don't know." That might even be the first step in self-honesty and self-discovery. Trying to always be right or make an impression— that's the ego's play, demanding attention. Let it go.

Don't be afraid to drop all grandiosity and just be empty. This can be an exceptionally hard teaching to incorporate because we all want to be someone, to become something great. Yet in true spirituality, we must be *nothing*. We must be willing to be entirely empty—of our ego.

If someone thinks they know a lot because they have practiced meditation for 50 years and have read 2500 books, there will be little openness to what is being shared here, and above all, little openness to catch the ego and realize its true non-existence (no-self).

I don't care whether you are 15 years old or 90 years old; whether you have practiced spirituality for 50 years or you're just starting; whether some great master initiated you, or even if you are a skeptic. That's all meaningless. Sri Ramana Maharshi got enlightened when he was 16 years old after a couple of minutes of Self-Inquiry. A beginner with no previous meditation experience doesn't mean he or she is far away from being enlightened. For example, it's possible that the "beginner's" spiritual maturity can actually be dormant such that they can quickly advance to a high level. It would not be the first time I've seen it. We need to have a broader vision and recognize that a person's "spiritual history" is not confined to this lifetime.

Just as with race or gender, age is absolutely unrelated to spiritual maturity or enlightenment.

Now, I have a confession to make. In life, I've interacted with a multitude of persons, from lawyers to university professors, sportspersons, politicians, and so on. Most of them had an incredibly strong attachment to their ego, which magnified the most egoistical facets of their personalities with traits such as deception, pride, greed, arrogance, egotism and superiority complexes. Yet despite that, the people who I've seen with the biggest ego-delusion and the most hardcore ego self-perseverance mechanisms were "spiritual people."

Why am I telling you this? So that you don't fall into the same trap. Whenever you dive deep into spirituality, you must proceed with extreme caution, being always alert so that your ego doesn't acquire a *supernatural ability* to preserve and defend itself.

You must drink from the high-discernment antidote in order to become immune to the ego's self-deception tricks.

Obviously, dwelling too much on the ego will only reinforce its presence. Yet, without opening your eyes to what the ego can do "behind your back," you will never go beyond it.

Have you ever read a spiritual book that you initially thought was just okay, but then months or years later read that very same book and got "Wowed"? Did the book change? Did the teachings change? No. You just became spiritually more mature. Every time someone becomes spiritually more mature[11], the ego blocks less and less, and one

---

[11] Being spiritually more mature is meant in an authentic way, such as being able to clearly discriminate what one once couldn't, e.g., between genuine and pure teachings versus false ego-based teachings. Being able to do out-of-body projections, seeing auras or talking with spirits are *not* signs of being spiritually more mature, just of having developed mental faculties.

can see what one couldn't see before. Being capable of looking at the ego and its mechanisms of survival is a sure sign of high spiritual maturity.

If you've made it thus far in this book, you have a higher than average spiritual maturity. The ego might not like it, but you know what? It can talk all it wants—we're just not listening anymore. Enough is enough!

CHAPTER **8**

SPIRITUALITY CAN BE THE EGO'S PLAYGROUND

The ego can easily turn a genuine seeker's spiritual efforts into a means of self-preservation. For example, one month you are practicing Kundalini Yoga, the next one you've moved on to the Buddhist meditation *anapanasati*, then you come back to Kundalini Yoga, but after two weeks you switch over to Kriya Yoga. Finally, you read a book about *Kabbalah* and its mystical and esoteric visualizations, and you start practicing it, which lasts ten weeks before going back to Kriya Yoga's pranayama.

Has anything like that ever happened to you? The ego will not let you pick just one spiritual system and follow it toward the very end. It is always looking for a change, for new techniques, new procedures, new methods and new teachings. A conflicted mind prevents the aspirant from adequately establishing a practice schedule and sticking to it.

Jumping from one teaching to another means you never dive deep enough, always staying on the surface. The example doesn't have to be as extreme as the aforementioned, but it can be as simple as constantly adding new components to your practice before having stabilized in the current stage. Even if you force yourself to stay with the same sadhana, in the back of your mind you might be thinking that it's not working and that you'll have to change it soon. A sincere practitioner needs to commit at least six months to their chosen practice before making informed and mature conclusions. Only after about six months can one know if the method chosen is working or not. And even then, it can be slightly misleading; it's not a set-in-stone rule. Besides, it depends on a multitude of factors such as your natural predisposition to certain types of practices, or whether you are practicing with total surrender versus mechanically.

How can you then know if you are making any progress or not?

If you feel more peaceful and joyful in your life than before, then that is a good measure. If your mind's chatter has diminished or if you are less identified with your ego, its thoughts, emotions, reactions, etc., that are happening on a day-to-day basis, then that is also a good sign. Breaking old patterns of conditioning, deprogramming mindless behaviors, being effortlessly more present throughout the day and dissolving deeply rooted, emotionally charged or traumatic events that were buried deep in the unconscious is another near-certain sign of progress.

However, these are still slightly subjective and cannot be taken for sure. Although they are generally true for the majority of the aspirants, there are instances where they are not. Sometimes you can be making progress and yet start to feel temporarily worse. For example, when an ingrained unconscious emotional contraction comes up to the conscious mind to be dissolved, you may feel uncomfortable and restless. That being said, if during such tumultuous period you stay mindful and don't get caught up in whatever pops up, you will reap immense benefits, profoundly reprogramming the way you feel about whatever emotional conditioning has surfaced from the depths of the unconscious. All that is required is an intense lucid awareness.

Contrary to popular belief, any type of "spiritual experience" is, for the most part, not a good indicator of progress. Here's an excerpt from *Kundalini Exposed* that explains this very well:

"You might go your whole sadhana without ever experiencing anything astonishingly 'mystical,' and in the last moment, the I-ego dissolves.

You might go your whole sadhana without ever experiencing anything astonishingly 'mystical,' and the I-ego might never dissolve.

You might go your whole sadhana full of spiritual experiences, and in the last moment, the I-ego dissolves.

You might go your whole sadhana full of spiritual experiences, and the I-ego might never dissolve.

You can never know.

Let me tell you a little secret:

The I-ego wants to preserve itself. If having spiritual experiences keeps it alive and healthy, that's precisely what it will allow you to experience.

If, on the other hand, not having any spiritual experiences will make you stop trying altogether, then that's what it will attempt to do.

Do you see it?

Having or not having any spiritual experience is not a proper evaluation of your spiritual progress. For all you know, tomorrow you might realize your true ever-present nature!

Progress may be indiscernible to the practitioner. The

mind going all over the place might be a sign of progress. How do you know? There are countless cases of people starting to practice, and having the usual 'monkey mind.' After one year of practicing, their mind is now peaceful every time they do their sadhana. One day, they sit down to practice and the mind scatters in a way that they've never experienced before. Now, every time they meditate, the mind is absolutely uncontrollable. They don't understand... what's going on? Let me tell you that this might actually be a sign of progress! There are cases that when you hit a certain threshold of depth in your practice, the ego will attempt anything to disrupt you. It knows its end might be near!

Never get discouraged, and *know* that if you are practicing the correct practices, as I have been sharing since Book 1 [Kriya Yoga Exposed], with true surrender and intent, then you'll undoubtedly make it all the way to the 'end.'"

Here's a quote from the Buddha saying exactly the same thing:

"All experiences are preceded by mind, having mind as their master, created by mind."

- DHAMMAPADA

Always remember:

Never practice with the intent to achieve any particular outcome, but rather because you enjoy and love practicing. It's a moment of joy and peace. Whatever is meant to happen will happen, and it will be for your good. Be persistent and go all the way. Nobody ever regretted being enlightened— it's the ultimate goal of every living being, even if they don't know it yet.

The ego is also the one who is always looking not just for spiritual experiences, but for "spiritual awakenings," "*samadhis*," "ecstasies," and so on, postulating a never-ending higher and higher state of consciousness. The truth is that as long as one is not completely fulfilled, one is still operating based on the egoic mind. Plus, every state of consciousness, no matter how profound or high it is, is always a mind-state, which means it's always a dualistic state.

Enlightenment is the end of the ego, the end of separation, the end of "I" and then subsequently "others," which means that no "higher" or "lower" state is possible, for what remains is only pristine primordial Awareness, the substratum of all states, no matter how gross and ignorant or subtle and mindful they are.

If we equate the ego to noise, and pure Awareness to silence, we can easily see how "higher and higher" states of consciousness are merely subtler and subtler forms of noise. Removing all the noise, only silence remains, which makes it *impossible* for any variation of higher or lower states to occur. This silence is undifferentiated, immutable and permanent. Pure Awareness is like a cinema screen, it doesn't move; only the movie—ego-noise—moves and goes to deeper or shallower states. The constant search for more, for a higher awakening or a deeper state of consciousness simply means that the seeking for complete fulfillment and realization still remains.

Reading countless spiritual books filled with dogmas and detours[12], and intellectualizing about the non-dual truth, is not realizing it either. Concepts, ideas, and thoughts are not the path to enlightenment—they are just more ego-noise. Do not forget this. The false self is hungry for such intellectual accomplishments, but runs away from whatever will bring it to its end.

There are spiritual systems that dwell too much on the workings of the mind, mapping out everything, attempting to theoretically detail every little step, as if one were doing a dissertation on "how to attain enlightenment." This is just another mind trap, but a subtler one. The spiritual ego loves

---

[12] ...which equate to 95% of the spiritual literature available today.

to explore all of the numerous manifestations of consciousness, always keeping "busy" and looking for "concrete and attainable spiritual goals," which are merely states of mind, albeit more refined than the normal waking consciousness.

The truth is that once you are aware of how dysfunctional and tricky your ego is, always causing suffering and a feeling of being unfulfilled, you will go right through all those elaborate intellectual labyrinths. Not that they might not be useful—in certain circumstances they are—but they can also easily pose as distractions that feed the ego, in a subtle and unconscious manner. This is especially true since the ego is always seeking something to attach itself to, so that it can reinforce its illusory sense of self.

Keeping the mind entertained in useless pursuits is also a way that the ego preserves itself (procrastination). The ego-mind would prefer to watch that TV show rather than read a profound spiritual book or meditate. Once it starts meditating, it begins to doze off. Even reading a profound spiritual book can suddenly turn into a yawning contest.

Of course one can and should enjoy life, but there is no greater enjoyment and bliss than finding out who you really are. Then, and only then, will life be truly filled with happiness and joy. As said in *The Secret Power of Kriya Yoga*, God is the pinnacle of happiness!

CHAPTER 9

REMAIN LIKE THE BUDDHA

What is the world that people see? The majority of humans are not truly aware of the world, but rather of the silent narrator in their heads that constantly grabs their attention.

This is particularly true if they stay in the same geographical region throughout their lives. They live on auto-pilot with a distorted and clouded awareness, judging, interpreting, labeling, and so on. Can you go on with your day and perceive without thinking, making conclusions, or trying to figure something out?

It's a good exercise to commit one day or a week to not labeling or making any conclusions about anything. Try it and see how your ego instantly tries to judge everything and everyone all the time.

Besides the constant judging and labeling, the ego is always ready to fight, especially against those who threaten it. If your mental self-image feels as if it's being "attacked," it will

THE YOGA OF CONSCIOUSNESS

quickly defend itself, either through finding excuses (a form of self-justification), or countering with criticism and condemning whoever it perceives to be the "attacker."

It doesn't matter whether what it is being said is true or false; you have to keep the ego on a short leash. Be fully aware, and allow what is being said to be expressed without feeling offended. Only your identity, which is something you are trying to get rid of, can be attacked—the real you can't. Knowing this, remain calm, being entirely aware of what is happening; do not lose awareness and don't let yourself be possessed by automatic and unconscious ego-defense mechanisms. Do not allow anger or any other kind of instant retaliation to occur. Remain like the Buddha, *fully calm, fully aware.*

Once, while the Buddha was giving a discourse in a city, an angry and displeased villager came to the lecture and started shouting, insulting and cursing at him. The villager was distraught because he had heard that someone from his clan, in the presence of the Buddha, had gone from being a householder to becoming a monk.

The Buddha simply asked the villager if he served guests food when receiving them at his house. Obviously, the angry man said yes, sometimes he did. Then the Buddha asked him if the guests reject the offer, to whom do those foods belong? It's not a surprise that if someone doesn't accept your gifts, they belong to you. In the same way, the Buddha didn't accept anything the angry man had tried to "gift him" (insults, cursing, etc.). He didn't react, for he did not get insulted, which meant those gifts stayed with the villager. When being non-reactive, negativity will always fall back on those who offer it, and they will be the only ones who become unhappy and dissatisfied[13].

If someone attacks or critiques you (your self-image), and you notice the ego starting to heat up, remember to remain completely aware, and make sure you pay special attention to how you feel within. Even if it's painful and agonizing, and many negative thoughts pop up, just allow them to be there without identifying with them. Don't suppress or struggle, just let them be.

It is easier said than done, but make an effort to be extremely alert in such situations. This level of lucid awareness will pay off big time in the long run. You will see that your sense of worth has not shrunk, but it's as if your awareness has expanded. Often, you will even see the situation happening in the "third-person," as if you were a speck of consciousness watching the scene occur from afar.

It is relatively manageable to do it with strangers or those

---

[13] *Akkosa Sutta: Insult*, translated from the Pali by Thanissaro Bhikkhu.

THE YOGA OF CONSCIOUSNESS

whose opinions we could care less about, but when it happens in situations related to loved ones or close friends, it's a lot harder. People get hurt or heartbroken when it happens with someone they're emotionally connected with[14].

This is a powerful spiritual practice—it's not just about sitting on the cushion. Mindfulness must be cultivated while both meditating and in our day-to-day life. As equanimity[15] arises in you, you will be able to respond to each situation with calmness and wisdom. By not allowing your ego to defend itself and by remaining non-reactive, you are not losing anything, becoming weaker or being humiliated—you are actually becoming stronger, purer, and wiser.

The ego will never recognize this because it sees it as a vulnerability. In fact, this is invincibility. It shows that you are not identifying with your fake sense of self, allowing the true sense of Self to shine "unobstructed." Of course, this doesn't mean you do nothing about the situation in question. There's no reaction, but you might need to take action. Non- reactivity is not a door to allow abuse or an invitation for others to run over you. Your actions and words can and

---

[14] Most of the time, when someone starts ranting against you, they are just projecting their current state of being onto you.

[15] Equanimity is a state where you don't react with desires or aversions to whatever happens, no matter how pleasant or distasteful that experience is. Regardless of the situation, you will never lose your composure and calmness.

will be assertive at times, but they will not be coming from a place of self-defense or self-justification.

After all, who can touch one who doesn't attempt to be anyone? You can touch something but you cannot touch nothing. You cannot hurt space, not even with a nuclear bomb.

When equanimity is in full force, you cannot be touched, yet you pervade everything—you are like infinite space.

PART II – THE TRUE SELF

CHAPTER **10**

WITHOUT ANYTHING, I STILL AM

Everything that you can experience or know is known through awareness. Even if in their ignorance, people consider the "I" to be the body and personality, with its story and traits, the awareness that pervades all experience is what we truly refer to as "I."

What is it exactly that knows this "I"? The "I" itself. It is the "I" that knows itself, not as an object but merely by being. Just like the eyes cannot directly see themselves, a knife cannot cut itself, or a scale cannot weigh itself, the subject cannot know itself. Yet you know the eyes exist by the mere fact that you can see[16], the knife by the mere fact that it cuts and the scale by the mere fact that it weighs. In the same way, you know the subject exists by the mere fact that you

---

[16] Yes, you can see them in a mirror, but that's only a reflection, not the "real thing." In the same way, you can see the subject in the objects, which is the only way the Absolute (non-duality) can "see" itself (through the mirror of duality).

exist, that you are aware. No object tells you this—it's your own ability to be aware of them that shows that the subject, awareness, exists. The subject knows itself *merely by being, by being aware.*

Although the subject and the world both seem to exist separated from each other, it doesn't mean that's actually the truth. We are mistaking a rope for a snake, and although the snake-illusion really seems to be there, it's still a rope.

As long as there seems to be a subject that perceives a world, there also seems to be a world to be perceived. They appear and subside in the space of consciousness simultaneously. Without a perceiving subject, there can be no perception; hence, without anything being perceived, there can't be a perceiver, since both are dependent on each other.

Whenever the "I" rises, form rises with it, and perceiving happens. Without experiencing some form, the "I" cannot rise. That's why the most potent spiritual practice is trying to find the "I-ego," and abide in that "I-ness" (which is the background of consciousness) in the absence of everything else, melting it. Duality (subject<->object) will then melt as well.

The problem is that finding that "I" is not as easy as it seems for most aspirants. Continuously being attached to and identified with many different objects, from the personality to memories, prevents consciousness from finding and abiding in the real sense of being, of "I am," often mistaking some sensation or feeling for it.

That's why at first, seekers of the Truth require a clear understanding of what "I" is not. That's the purpose of applying the so-called Witness Stage.

We could go on and practice *neti-neti*, which means "neither this, nor that," which is a practice where "I" realizes that it is neither a particular object, nor another, and so on, until no objects are left for the consciousness to identify itself with, remaining objectless and pure. Removing everything, what remains is *What Is*.

The issue with *neti-neti* is that it is no more than an intellectual practice for most, making it not particularly helpful beyond gaining a mental understanding of what "I" is not. Someone can intellectually know that "the body is not I," yet that doesn't mean they know it on an *experiential* level.

The way to realize that "I" is not whatever object it is identified with, is to experience directly that awareness, which is what "I" points toward, remains even in the absence of that object.

There are different levels of such minor realizations, for example:

THE YOGA OF CONSCIOUSNESS

You might say "I am angry" whenever thoughts and feelings of anger arise in you. But are you really angry, or are you just identifying with thoughts and feelings that you call "anger"? Are those thoughts and feelings appearing in the space of awareness? Don't you perceive them? You witness them appear and eventually disappear. That means you stand apart from them. You perceive those feelings and thoughts of anger.

Whenever you are watching a movie or reading a fiction book that you really enjoy, you connect with its characters— you feel their emotions, their feelings, and their state of mind. You can become so engrossed in that movie or book that you become emotionally attached to it. You suffer when the characters suffer, you laugh when they laugh, you are happy when they are happy, etc. You, *consciousness*, are so engrossed in the movie of your life that you become extremely identified with whatever pops up in the space of awareness.

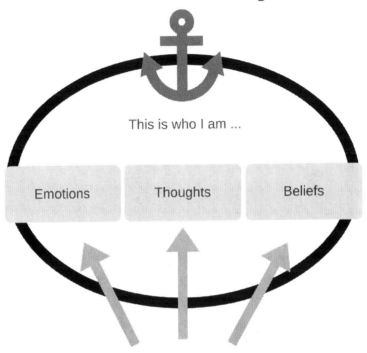

If someone broke your smartphone in half, would you say "You just broke me in half!"? Well, if your smartphone meant a lot to you, then you'd probably say so, but if not, you'd say "You just broke my smartphone in half!" You saw someone breaking your smartphone in half. You, consciousness, witnessed someone break your smartphone, an object, in half. In the same way, if you pay close attention, especially when such situations occur, you will realize that you, consciousness, witness the thoughts and feelings of anger, which are objects, appear (not with your eyes obviously, but with your innate ability to perceive).

Do you see it? If so, then don't identify with it. Whatever you can see is not you. By seeing that thoughts and feelings of anger come up, and then subside, you have the clear direct realization that they cannot be you. They cannot even touch you! You are witnessing them untouched. You just had never examined yourself closely enough before, because you were only looking at the surface, identifying with it, and believing it to be you.

Now, through impersonally perceiving, and without immersing in the false-self's constructs, you see all these phenomena appear and disappear, gaining some "space" and "lightness" in-between. This spaciousness allows the subject to finally breathe fresh air, unpolluted by the heavy objects it usually identifies with, realizing they are ephemeral and empty.

Consciousness starts disidentifying with its illusory self-image

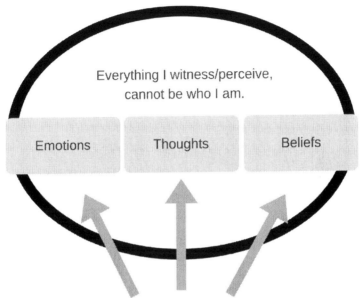

Everything I witness/perceive, cannot be who I am.

Emotions · Thoughts · Beliefs

WITNESSING/PERCEIVING WITHOUT ATTACHMENT WILL PURIFY THE "I," CREATING DISPASSION AND BREAKING THE PULL OF THOUGHTS, EMOTIONS, ETC.

I-ego

Witnessing

Such minor Insights are the beginning of something greater. There will come a time when you realize that all that appears in the space of awareness that we usually call "I" is but a mere object being perceived by your consciousness!

Without thoughts, I still am. Without memories, I still am. Without emotions, I still am. Without my personality, I still am. Without the five senses, I still am. Without the body, I still am. Without life-force, I still am. Without the mind, I still am. Without the intellect, I still am. Without the ego, I still am.

I still am what? *Aware.* I still am aware. I still exist. I am aware and exist without any of those "once-thought-to-be-I" adjuncts. But here's the kicker: I still am... without "I." An "I-less" I. Just I-less Awareness. That's what remains when whatever can be lost is lost. The Beingness that Awareness Is.

CHAPTER 11

DON'T RESIST LIFE

Growing up, we create a mental self-image built upon our conditioning. Usually, we are so busy with our life and our little self-centered corner that we get into problems, depression, and fears that we have no idea how we got in to. Becoming aware of our conditioning can be one of the first steps in understanding ourselves.

Our ego-mind is always worried about keeping our past and current story alive. Without our personal story, without our past, who are we? Waking up with total amnesia would be the end of "us" as we know ourselves to be—no personal narrative that defines our identities, no memories, no joyful past experiences, but also no past problems that used to haunt us either.

Impersonally witnessing the contents of our mind, with mindfulness, will bring the same nonattachment to the personal story, traumas, problems, etc., that amnesia brings, although without having to forget about them. It's like they happened to someone else, not to you, or as if they had occurred in a dream.

Your current actions will no longer be based on past conditioning, rather they will be spontaneous and in synchrony with the universe. The present is no longer seen either through the eyes of the past or as a bridge toward some apparent future where everything you want will be accomplished.

If you have created an unhappy self out of your life-story, and believe that this illusion is who you are, then, unconscious fear of letting your identity go might form a strong opposition to ego dis-identification.

You have to witness this resistance from a distance. Being conscious and lucidly observing it whenever you see it flaring up will eventually break its power and pull over you. Staying as the impersonal witness is essential for that to happen.

The mind itself is a great tool; it is not the problem. The problem is when you search for a sense of self in it, which you will never find. However, you might be tricked into believing that a personal self is there, which is but an illusion. Such a belief is built on a foundation made of thin air, prevailing only due to ignorance, which just means you haven't investigated deeply enough into your own mind.

By reading this book, you've already started a much deeper investigation than you've probably ever done before, and understanding how the Witnessing or Mindful Perceiving happens is the next vital step.

WITNESSING

To prevent the ego from blocking your dis-identification with your illusionary self, you have to be very aware throughout the day, as has been mentioned throughout the book so far. This teaching must be deeply infused into your consciousness.

Every time a bad situation happens, you must step back and witness everything. Not just the situation, but most importantly what happens within you—your mind, emotions, thoughts, reactions, etc.

Let's see a practical example:

John is a 30-year-old investment banker in New York City. He has a highly stressful yet well-paid job, working 15 hours per day, six days per week. He's been working like that for the past couple of years without time off, and finally, this year, he has two weeks to go on vacation with his family.

For the past two years he's been jealous that his long-time

friends have gone to Brazil during Christmas, and spent time on the beautiful beach of *Copacabana*, all while he had to stay working late hours in his office. This Christmas will be different. John is finally going to enjoy a long-awaited vacation on Brazilian beaches while New York is freezing.

When the time finally comes, an unexpected storm hits New York and grounds all of the scheduled flights to Brazil. John is heartbroken. He had been waiting for this day for such a long time, and now the opportunity is gone. He becomes depressed and passes the two weeks at home, drinking and binge-watching TV shows and movies. Afterward, he comes back to work and everything stays the same.

This was a rather depressing story, but one must see that one has no control over the weather. High expectations can often bring disappointment. If someone is going to get upset over what they have no control over, that is bound to happen.

Hold on a second. Let me repeat that.

If someone is going to get upset over what they have no control over... disappointment is sure to happen? Well, yes. But isn't this everyone's daily life? Well, yes—it's crazy.

People are getting angry and upset all day long because of circumstances that occur outside of their control. Isn't that insane?

Now, you're probably asking: what should one do in John's situation instead?

The first thing to do is to understand that everything that happens to you is for your "spiritual evolution"—even if you don't see it yet. Everything that happens to you is for your journey-less journey home. Don't resist what happens, whatever it is. This doesn't mean that if someone tries to steal your wallet, you let him—no. It just means to stop asking "Why me?", "Why is this happening to me?", "Why do I have such bad luck..." Stop making your ego the center of the world.

Emotionally allow everything that happens to you. Accept everything life gives you. Be glad for everything life sends your way. How often, on later analysis, do we realize that "Wow, that thing that happened to me long ago, that at the time I thought was awful, now I see it was actually great!"

The end of a relationship or losing a job can be the beginning of a new life, for example.

In John's example, little did he know that near Copacabana beach, during the time he was supposed to be there with his family, at the same hotel where he was supposed to stay, two robbers attacked and assaulted ten people, and three of them ended up passing away as a result. Perhaps, unbeknownst to him, the storm had just saved his life!

It is important to remember that nothing external has to change, only the way you feel about what happens.

Whenever a thought appears in your mind, don't cling to it. What happens when someone doesn't cling to a thought is that the thought returns to where it came from—emptiness. Thoughts come from "spaciousness" or "emptiness," but when you cling to them, they gain strength and end up materializing into your living reality. This is where *The Secret* or *The Law of Attraction* come from. Strongly visualizing and identifying with a thought, over and over again, will eventually turn it into your reality. All your actions, emotions, thinking patterns, beliefs, etc., will end up manifesting according to the thoughts that you keep focusing on repetitively. But this is still ignorance, still dreaming, still clinging to something external hoping it will bring peace, fulfillment, happiness and completeness. It will not. This subtle manipulation of reality is but a comfy self-imprisonment.

When we strongly yet unconsciously cling to a thought, it will also shape our life, but rather than being a pleasant dream, it could be a nightmare of suffering.

Before being able to impersonally perceive or witness the contents of your mind and whatever arises in your life, you need to have some degree of stillness and mind clarity.

That's why practicing some form of attention-based meditation is first required, such as Kriya Yoga, Kundalini Yoga, Buddhism, etc. That's the preliminary step, one that John's life eventually took him toward, which can all be traced back to the day he found out about the deadly assault in Brazil, two months later. How grateful he was for that unexpected storm! It has now transformed into a memorable day for John, but for good reasons!

CHAPTER **12**

THE POWER OF CONSCIOUS WITNESSING

Everyone starts meditating with a meditation object. Some esoteric traditions begin by fixing the gaze on a candle, or by visualizing simple letters or complex images. Others use a mantra, the breath sensations, prana, and so on. Every single one of these traditions starts with grosser objects, and then as the practice deepens and the aspirant's ability to sustain attention increases, proceeds to subtler and subtler objects of perception.

There's a high chance you've already practiced some form of energetic object-based practice, like Kriya Yoga, Kundalini Yoga, Buddhism or whatever it is. If you have read my previous books, there's also a chance you've been reposing in the "Self-Awareness," "just Being" or "I Am-ness" state. This is also called *Parvastha* in Kriya Yoga, and refers to the after-practice absorption state.

If you've already been doing that, it's amazing, and you are well ahead of most aspirants. If not, now it's the perfect time to start.

Yet, the rest of your time must be filled with conscious awareness, with presence. This can be called *The Power of Conscious Witnessing.*

Uniting the time spent meditating on-cushion, with consciously witnessing the ego off-cushion (and catching it whenever it tries to take control of your awareness), will accelerate your spiritual progress a million times.

Not only does *The Power of Conscious Witnessing* create space between you and what you used to identify with, but it helps to awaken discrimination between the subject and the object, or as it is written in many ancient scriptures, between the seer and the seen.

> "To overcome the outward-turning power of the mind is hard to accomplish without completely eliminating the veiling effect, but the covering over one's inner Self can be removed by discriminating between seer and objects."

> - VIVEKACHUDAMANI, ADI SANKARA

Doing sitting practices for one hour twice a day is not enough. What about the other 22 hours? Even if you were to discount the time you spend sleeping, there are still 14 hours left. It's like saying you want to stop eating meat, but you only change the breakfast from bacon and eggs to oatmeal. If you still eat a big steak at lunch, grab a ham sandwich in the afternoon, and have a lobster dinner, you are still eating meat.

It's not about doing some sitting practices and calling it a day. You must go further. Be aware throughout the day, witnessing everything that happens outside and within, without identifying with anything. Although it might seem complicated at first, it will get easier, and you'll naturally start doing it throughout the day.

Whenever you feel like you are off track, which will happen often, just come back to being aware. It's not a big deal, and don't get frustrated over it. With time, as you experience more peace and joy inside, you'll remember to do it more often. This will also create dispassion toward thoughts, emotions, and all the ephemeral objects of the world, which you will increasingly recognize for their futility and impermanence. It's like you've been so engrossed in a dramatic movie that you've completely lost awareness that you are merely watching a movie. Now, you are coming back to life.

The discernment between the objects and the seer (subject, witnessing consciousness) will come with full force.

In the after-effect of sitting practices, you are only paying attention to the background screen, the substratum aware-ness, being Self-Aware. During the day, you may be watching the movie, but you are consciously doing it in a way so that you don't get hypnotized by it. That will allow you to live an unworried and free life, and both should be combined.

> "The settling of the mind in its goal, by running away from the mass of objects through observing their de-fects again and again is known as peace."

> \- Vivekachudamani, Adi Sankara

Remember that until you outgrown the energetic and Kundalini-related practices, they must not be neglected. They are the rocket fuel that allows us to quickly fly toward the clear space of awareness and abide there. They are important and definitely have their role. Energetic/object-based practices, unattached witnessing and Self-Awareness practices work together toward a common goal.

Many teachers these days, like the Kriya Yoga Gurus, teach only energetic/object-based practices, disregarding the post-state mindful awareness. That's why their disciples don't "attain" enlightenment. Others, such as the modern *Advaita* teachers (usually called *Neo-Advaita*) teach that no practice whatsoever is necessary. Obviously, I don't find that correct. If you don't do anything to remove the ego-cloud that's seemingly obscuring the sun of Consciousness, it will remain like that. It is not enough to know intellectually that you are the sun and not the cloud. That certainly does not eliminate suffering nor the sense of being an individual.

Effort is truly necessary. Not only I, but many Gurus, Sages, and Masters have said the same:

"There is a state beyond our efforts or effortlessness. Until it is realized, effort is necessary."

"Effort is needed so long as there is mind."

"All efforts are for eliminating the present obscuration of the Truth."

- TALKS WITH SRI RAMANA MAHARSHI

"With all the earnest effort to be free from the bondage of the world, the wise must strive themselves."

- VIVEKACHUDAMANI, ADI SANKARA

"You yourself must strive. The Buddhas only point the way."

- DHAMMAPADA, THE BUDDHA

Effort doesn't equate with strenuous forcing, like the effort you would exert running the last mile of a marathon. It must be smart effort, like guiding a monkey back to its tree with the smell of a banana rather than catching it and chaining it forcefully. One can never permanently control the monkey with a chain. When it is set loose, it will run. On the other hand, with smart handling, the monkey will love you and do whatever you wish, since you provide exactly what it wants—bananas.

Mastery of the mind is a very tough and complicated subject. Can you ever have complete mind-control? It is the mind that is attempting to control itself, and you cannot "brute-force" your way toward enlightenment.

Through those yogic practices, the mind can be brought under control for a while (e.g., when breathlessness[17] is achieved), but then it will go back to its standard behavior.

---

[17] Breathlessness is called *Kevala Kumbhaka*. When the in-breath merges with the out-breath, through some yogic practices, they cancel each other and breathlessness occurs. Lots of Kriya Yoga aspirants make it a goal, which makes it harder to achieve, always looking for an outcome and becoming unsatisfied or restless if it doesn't happen. I have found that a better strategy is to not place much emphasis on it. If it happens, fine, if it doesn't, fine as well. In the later stages of your practice, you are supposed to be focused on your own awareness, and if you are aware of being breathless or not is irrelevant, and can actually become a slight distraction, since you are diverting your attention toward the breath. Know that if the breath has to stop, it will stop on its own, even during the after-practice state, while you might remain unaware of that.

That is why discernment is so hugely needed, yet at the same time it's highly misunderstood and overlooked. The ego needs to realize that the best thing it can do is to search for its self-existence. The ego is a junction between pure Consciousness and the body. Its essence (the conscious part) is what is real, eternal, and never-lacking.

Whenever we perceive objects, we are strengthening the mind's outer attention, which is temporary (waking and dream states). Whenever we repose as "I am," we are abiding in the "aware" part of the mind which will make it lose the "otherness" part, the dynamic consciousness (objects/ forms) part, leaving only the eternal empty awareness (static consciousness). The mind must understand that all of the happiness, bliss, peace, and completeness that it is searching for can only be found within, in its own source.

With a real awakened discernment, you will not have a difficult time "controlling" the mind because the mind itself understands that it wants to dissolve and realize its true nature as bliss Consciousness. It will not be you against the ego-mind, but both will play on the same team. The mind will happily drown in bliss.

Laboring with the breath is semi-effective. It is the first step given to beginners because the breath, prana, and the mind are all interconnected, the latter being a subtler form of the previous.

103

Controlling the mind	Hard.
Controlling the prana	Semi-hard.
Controlling the breath	Achievable.

By controlling the breath, we control prana, and we end up controlling the mind. Yet this does not lead to Freedom. As you know, there will come a time when all practices (movements of the mind) must be let go of, so that we can abide in the source of mind itself ("I" or "I am"—depending on which tradition you're familiar with).

If you find that your mind is too wild for you to properly perform this "observing" or "witnessing" practice, or that there's too much mind-wandering, "monkey-mind," dullness or drowsiness, then you should do some purifying practices such as Kriya Yoga (as explained in Kriya Yoga Exposed), or Kundalini Yoga (as explained in Kundalini Exposed) first. By doing these purifying practices first, they will enable you to do the witnessing or observing practice afterward with a stable attention that will prevent identification with whatever arises in your consciousness at any time.

It is time to trust in yourself. Not in the ego-self, but in your real Self. By turning within and learning how to be with your own Self, Awareness, you will come to know who you truly are.

CHAPTER **13**

RECOGNIZE THE BACKGROUND

We all readily accept that we are in the waking state with a body, thoughts, feelings, etc., which we consider to be "real." In the dream state, it is the same—we have a body, thoughts, feelings, etc., and we consider them to be "real" during the dream, but "unreal" after waking up. But when we move on to the deep dreamless sleep state, there is nothing, no body, no thoughts, no feelings, just nothing. We don't consider it real or unreal since it's not a period registered by our minds.

When we go to sleep, everything is let go of—everything is abandoned. Unless we abandon everything, we cannot fall asleep. Even if your soulmate or child is sleeping next to you, you have to let go of him or her as well. The waking state has to be dropped in order to fall asleep.

In deep dreamless sleep, peace and happiness are abundant. Imagine you are really tired after a long day. Notice how pleasant and peaceful it feels when you go to sleep. That's merely a prelude.

However, you can say: "But I'm not aware during deep dreamless sleep!"

Well, are you really sure? Something was awake because you know you didn't think about anything during deep dreamless sleep; you know that there was nothing there, just peaceful emptiness. You were aware of that nothingness.

There has to be a distinction here:

The ego-mind[18], the personality, is the one that falls asleep at night. That person has no memory of sleep. The body closes its eyes, has a loss of awareness of space-time, and then, in the morning, opens its eyes, and everything continues as it was left. But deeper than the superficial ego-personality, there is an impersonal witness that saw the fading out of objects, and the "blackness" that occurred[19]. Then, it knew "nothing." It also witnessed the fading in of dream-objects, and their fading out into oblivion. This process repeats itself multiple times throughout the night.

---

[18] Ego-mind = ego ("I") and mind (ego's adjuncts/accumulated characteristics, such as name, likes, dislikes, memories, beliefs, etc.).

[19] It is not "blackness," but this is the perception that the mind has of that no-mind "moment," because it was a "blank." There were no objects nor anything conceivable by the mind.

In the morning, it witnesses the fading in of the waking-state-world and the respective body-personality.

Yet, human beings are rarely aware of this background witness. It is unattached to anything, and merely witnesses whatever comes and goes. The body's personality is what fades out at night and appears in the morning. Abiding in this witness is one of the ways to disassociate from the "personhood," thus dissolving it and achieving Liberation.

PURIFYING THE "I"

Usually, when an aspirant is practicing and the mind starts becoming still, unconscious processes begin to come up to the conscious mind. This is well known by everyone who has done even just a little bit of meditation.

"How come that long-forgotten memory, painful experience or emotional trauma has appeared in my mind out of nowhere?" This is a natural purification process. Typically, practitioners ignore such thoughts, emotions or images and keep practicing what they were practicing. However, sometimes, those surfacing "troublesome contents" are too strong to ignore and they powerfully capture our attention.

This might happen a lot during the post-practice state because that's the moment when your mind is the quietest. Investigating such "objects" serves no purpose, but if they simply can't be ignored, it is best to just witness them without being "pulled in," without identifying with them, without thinking about them or trying to "figure them out.". Rather than rejecting them, allow them to be, for they represent occult parts of your mind that need to be acknowledged, accepted and let go of. Try your best to objectively perceive whatever pops up, without allowing yourself to get caught up in it. Remember that regardless of whichever emotion appeared in your mind, it's only an object appearing in the space of awareness, and it will dissolve if *it is not repressed*. Don't judge yourself or feel guilty in any way. Just remain fully lucid, and the cultivation of non-grasping and equanimity will spontaneously occur.

During the day, witnessing occurs naturally, perceiving whatever happens both within and without, while always trying to stay non-reactive and lucidly aware, never condemning others or yourself. You can even do it while working, if your work doesn't depend too much on the intellect, or if you are not doing something dangerous like operating heavy machinery. Use your discernment.

Every time you manage to stay mindful throughout the day, presently aware, and always speaking, acting and living mindfully, you are purifying your "I" by deprogramming your unconscious habits and tendencies that you've accumulated. As the obsolete programming fades, you will become more awake, lucid, and your actions will always come from your deepest sense of being rather than from the ego. Your "I" will become so transparent and pure that it will eventually disappear, along with its sense of separateness and incompleteness.

THE YOGA OF CONSCIOUSNESS

WHAT I ONCE CONSIDERED TO BE "I," WHICH WAS UNCONSCIOUSLY CONTROLLING ME, HAS NO LONGER POWER.

Consciousness is anchored in the witnessing "I"

PURIFIED "I-EGO"

CHAPTER 14

FREEDOM IS NOT AN OBJECT OF MEDITATION

Developing stable attention is fundamental. Concentration is one of the most important abilities, not just in meditation but in life. Hence, it's no surprise that spiritual traditions put a lot of importance on developing attention and one-pointedness. This can be quite a challenge for meditators, especially beginners, since these days, humans seem to lack any kind of stable attention. We could even say the majority of humans have an attention deficit disorder (ADD), often finding a solution in pills.

Although pills may temporarily fix the attention problem, they can bring terrible long-term side-effects. Meditation is a better a solution, and is becoming more mainstream (but is still utilized way less than Big Pharma's provided solutions).

Training the attention using techniques like anapanasati,

mantras, chakra-focus, pranayama, and so on, can bring immense benefits, both spiritual and more "mundane." Yet being a great meditator doesn't necessarily mean that one is liberated.

Studying the mind and dwelling on deep mind states is definitely interesting, but does not lead to Liberation—it can actually raise an impenetrable wall.

Practices that involve abiding in awareness (i.e. being Self-attentive, the Parvastha of Kriya Yoga, or meditating on the "I am") are unlike all other practices because they don't rely on a subject placing attention on an object. True non-dual practice is not a mental state, because it does not use objects. It is subject/awareness based. It's not a doing, but a being.

Object-based practices can never lead to Liberation because they are dualistic. They are important as a preparatory practice. When aspirants egoically defend their spiritual tradition as being the best, they are actually being ignorant. No matter how different their practice is, they all do similar things in the long run. One is not better than the other; they merely suit a particular aspirant's temperament and innate abilities better.

There's no "reaching out," "attaining" or "accomplishing" a goal when one abides in the background of consciousness. It is just being still with your whole being, while remaining aware. When practiced regularly by an aspirant with a properly matured mind, it will strip off all of the subtle remaining conditioning and desires.

Rather than paying attention to what is temporary and mutable (objects), and therefore unreal, we pay attention to what is eternal and immutable (pure empty consciousness), and therefore real.

Despite the importance of the abovementioned, and in alignment with what has been shared in the previous books, many still disregard it and focus on the techniques to the exclusion of the "Just Being" after-state.

Usually, people think that "Just Being" is very abstract and hard to follow, from a practical standpoint. They prefer the complicated technical and mechanical processes of a "normal" spiritual practice. "It's not practical," "It's philosophical." These statements are not a surprise. The ego would rather do techniques and mind movements which keep aspirants in the realm of the mind than go beyond it. It's truly an ego-deception.

"Just Being" is much more powerful than what the mind would have you believe. Although it might start off as an "I" actively focusing upon itself, and seem like a "doing," it will eventually stop being an "I" inside a spacious impersonal Presence, and will evolve into an impersonal Presence-

Beingness being itself. This is the transition from duality to non-duality—a going from "trying to just be" or "trying to be aware of awareness" or "trying to do nothing" to actually "just being," "aware of awareness," "doing nothing," respectively.

Post-practice awareness is the most essential part of any real sadhana, and yet it is the one that gets neglected the most. Unbeknownst to most practitioners, this "state," on its own, will also:

1. Collect all of the prana into the central canal;

2. Open the Sushumna Nadi;

3. Awaken the Kundalini;

4. Raise it all the way to the Crown Chakra;

5. Melt it into the Spiritual Heart.

It's so simple that the mind will never give it its deserved recognition. If you skip this Self-Awareness state, you will never achieve Liberation. Kriya, Kundalini or any other techniques on their own will never lead you all the way to Self-Realization.[20]

---

[20] Yet both are essential. Authentic spiritual traditions will incorporate both. Kriya Yoga does it with Pranayama & other techniques + Parvastha. Kundalini Yoga as taught in *Kundalini Exposed* does it with Kriya Supreme Fire + The Beingness After-state; Buddhism does it with Samatha + Vipassana; and so on.

ALTHOUGH THE OLD "ME" CAN STILL, AT TIMES, FLARE UP, IT NO LONGER POSES AS AN OBSTACLE. HENCE, THERE IS NO LONGER THE NEED TO WITNESS ANYTHING, BUT RATHER JUST BE; THE "I" JUST PAYS ATTENTION TO ITSELF. NO NEED TO DISIDENTIFY WITH ANYTHING, BUT JUST MELT IN ITS OWN AWARENESS.

The witnessing "I" tries to witness itself. The final step to a truly non-dual practice

SELF-ABIDANCE

Spirituality is not about attending to otherness. It is about attending to the source of otherness. The source of otherness is "I," since only after an "I" arises, does otherness appear. Attending to "I" dissolves otherness, which inevitably means it dissolves "I" as well. Without the constraints of "I," Freedom Is. The ultimate object of meditation is the subject itself! That's true spirituality!

CHAPTER 15

UNDERSTANDING THE FOUNDATION OF SPIRITUAL PRACTICE

Since your attention is one of your most precious innate abilities, where you direct it, so your life and consciousness flow. Put your attention on attention itself, correctly and often enough, and see how everything melts in bliss!

You can direct your attention to external objects, breathing, mantras, visualizations, chakras, energy, life-force, and so on, but by now you ought to know that these practices are just a preliminary step. However, by focusing your attention on attention itself, on the background, you will be led directly to the fountain you've been searching for—the fountain of eternal bliss. Reposing on this background is much more important that it might sound.

In the next chapter there will be instructions that are like pointers to direct your attention exclusively to the background of consciousness. The background of consciousness

THE YOGA OF CONSCIOUSNESS

is the subject, the witness, and the substratum of all perceptions and experiences. That's where you have to abide.

These instructions can be said to be "non-dual practices" that help you trigger the Self-Awareness state back if you "drop" out of it. If you are practicing some form of yoga, your practice will lead you to this Self-Awareness after-state in the end, and it can last anywhere from one single second up to days. The permanent Self-Awareness state, the effortless natural state of pure blissful Being, is our true enlightened nature.

All of these objectless meditations will lead you to the direct experience of who you are, rather than filling your mind with ideas, definitions, and concepts about who you are. At the end of the day, you don't want words, practices or pointers. You want the truth. You want yourself. Only that will truly fulfill you.

These should only be done after the aspirant has developed sufficient discrimination between objects (what is perceivable; including objects of the mind, such as thoughts) and the subject (impersonal witness, that which witnesses everything, even thoughts). Such discrimination is developed by practicing as was explained in the previous chapters. Additionally, one needs to have reached a natural and easily accessible state of abiding as the witness, so that one can correctly recognize the background of consciousness, the state of Presence, the subject, and abide there, without focusing on any objects.

There's a difference between doing a Self-Awareness practice naturally at the end of your routine (or as a standalone practice whenever you wish), versus trying to do it when you're active throughout the day. While the first is the most powerful, because all of your attention, beingness and intention are being placed upon your own awareness exclusively, the latter cannot achieve this. For example, if you are eating dinner, your attention has to be split between the eating and your own awareness. That is why it's best to be fully Present as the impersonal unattached witness throughout your daily activities, letting what comes, come, what goes, go, and reserving the exclusive Self-attentiveness practice for when you are not doing anything else.

First

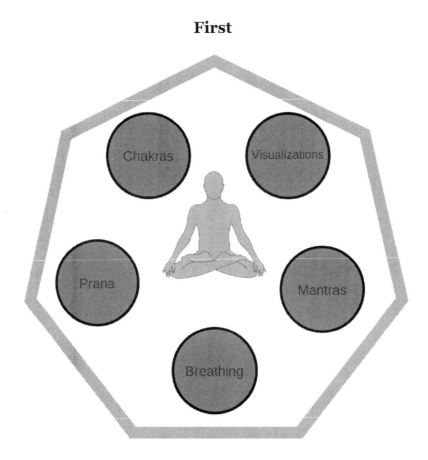

Subject practices with subtle objects

Then

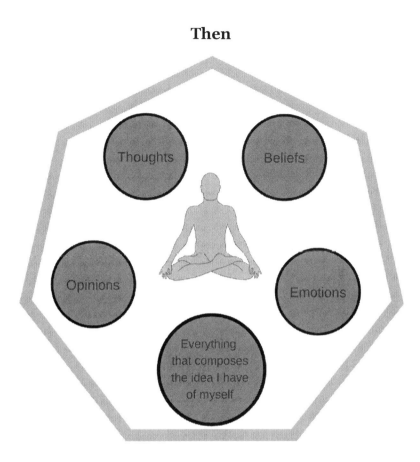

Subject breaks the identification with the thinking mind and all its facets that compose the "identity"

Finally

Subject abides in its subjectivity, breaking the subject-object dichotomy, meaning there is no longer object or subject. That's non-duality.

Energetic spiritual practices (*Shakti/Kundalini/Pranic* related) lead to an easy abidance in the witness, which in turn leads to the dis-identification with *rajasic* and *tamasic gunas* (attributes and tendencies not conducive to Self-Realization). Only *sattvic* (pure) qualities remain[21], which are the perfect ground for being Self-attentive, abiding in the background of consciousness to the exclusion of everything else.

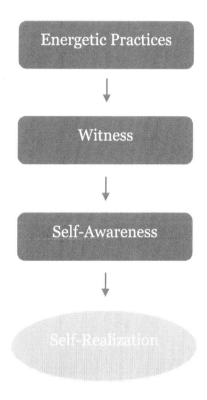

---

[21] Calm mind, intense desire for Liberation, honesty, kindness, etc.

The only difference between exclusively abiding in Self-Awareness and the Witness practice, is that in the Witness practice, consciousness is still witnessing something so that it can realize how everything is impermanent[22], empty[23] and "not I," while in Self-Awareness, the same witness stops paying attention to anything besides itself, as it has broken its self-identification with what was once thought to be "I" (e.g., personality).

The transition from witnessing to Self-Awareness is not a black and white, either-or switch. Often, there will be "gray" areas. For example, you are Self-aware (conscious of being conscious), then a thought or sensation pops up, causing you to lose Self-attentiveness and breaking your Self-Awareness. Yet you still stay as the subject, witnessing whatever appeared in the mind with nonattachment until it

---

[22] Consciousness realizes how everything is temporary. Nothing lasts, everything comes and goes. Ultimately, time dissolves everything. Recognizing the ephemeral nature of every person, object, state, experience, *everything*, creates dispassion, because attachment to what is temporary will undoubtedly lead to suffering.

[23] Consciousness realizes how everything is empty. Nothing has any value nor can it bring any happiness by itself. If things had happiness in themselves, everyone would feel contentment for the same objects, events, people, etc. As it is the experience of everyone that there are people who dislike what others enjoy, it is easy to deduce that happiness is inherent in every human being and not in the objects themselves. This Insight makes desire fall away, for it is recognized that nothing can provide that which one is looking for—everlasting happiness and unbroken completeness.

dissolves. Afterward, do not wait for another thought or object to appear, just go back to being aware of awareness; that is, exclusively Self-aware.

With practice, the "Witness-less just-Awareness" gaps will start happening for longer and longer periods of time, eventually reaching an effortless state where there's only non-dual Consciousness and no need to witness anything anymore[24].

Throughout your journey, the "I" will come back often, sometimes even stronger. Deep-rooted habits stemming from countless lifetimes, unconscious desires, fears, traumas, etc., all work against you. Yet, being persistent with your spiritual practice will unlock all of the unconscious debris, so that they come to the surface to be purified and realized as not self. However, as many things have yet to be manifested in your current life, still being in seed form, there will be times where you will be able to clear them without them being materialized or at least, without materializing too strongly.

---

[24] Ancient scriptures talk about Consciousness/Awareness being a "witness" because it facilitates the awakening of discrimination between the subject and object. When there are no objects, the witness alone remains, but without the witnessed, can there be any witness? No, its overlap on Awareness melts, and only Awareness is left, without even the witnessing "attribute."

Usually, this is the sadhana progression:

Ego-based practices, which bring stillness and lucidity and allow us to go to the witness stage;

Witness-based practices, which awaken the essential discernment and break the identification of consciousness with the ego's adjuncts in order to be able to abide on itself exclusively.

These will naturally and automatically result in:

Consciousness being conscious of itself, of its own formless non-dual Being. This is the final stage. The background of consciousness is no longer "the background," but just consciousness.

There is no distinction anymore between the background and the foreground. Subject and object dissolve, non-duality alone is. It only ever is.

CHAPTER **16**

PRACTICING NON-DUALITY

Here I will give direct practical instructions on how to abide in the "I am," the "Just Being" state, that you can put to use right away.

Use these instructions as guidelines. They have the purpose of leading you to what is prior to the mind—pure Consciousness. Although at first you can mentally guide yourself with these words, afterward, let them go and allow yourself to sink into an empty clear silent awareness.

When you get up, let the state of being that has been recognized within "follow" you throughout your day, expanding and pervading your whole life with beauty and joy.

These instructions are written in no particular order, but are listed alphabetically. They are written as simple and clear as possible, guiding your attention back to its source. Don't try to understand or logically analyze them, just literally follow the instructions. Read and try them all, and see which one allows you to more easily abide in your own sense of being, your own awareness. Allow at least 10 minutes per instruction when testing which one fits you best, "marinating" where it points you toward.

Like a dog chasing its tail, when the mind tries to grasp non-duality, it gets dizzy and can never accomplish it. Yet, once it becomes still, the dog can become aware that its tail is already its own. The mind just has to stop moving—once it becomes truly still, non-duality will be realized.

You can do these exercises whenever you wish. As said before, they are extremely useful at the end of your practice, when resting in the after-state, to help you abide longer and longer there (but you can do them anytime, even if just for 5 minutes when waiting for something, for example). Soon, bliss will surge up in your heart, expanding toward your whole being. Follow that bliss and be one with it.

Non-dual Instructions

Awareness

Be aware of being aware. Be aware of awareness itself. Be consciously aware of being consciously aware.

Not aware of thoughts, not aware of not having thoughts, but aware of being aware.

Blackness

Close your eyes and be aware of the blackness that you see. Now, rather than seeing that blackness, see the one that is looking behind your eyes. See the seer.

Conscious

Are you conscious? Notice that you are.

Keep noticing that you are conscious.

If you forget that you are conscious, as soon as you remember, gently come back to remembering that you are conscious.

Keep being conscious that you are conscious.

Dropping

Drop the idea of being a body. Drop the idea of being a person. Drop the idea of being someone. Drop the idea of wanting to be someone. Drop the idea of wanting to be somewhere. Drop all ideas. Drop all thoughts. Drop everything you can until there is nothing left to drop.

When there is nothing left to drop, drop the "Ok, now what?" that might appear in your mind.

What is left? Recognize it and stay there.

Forgetting

Forget about your body. It is illusory.

Forget about your mind. It is illusory.

Forget about the world. It is illusory.

Forget about the illusion. It is illusory.

Forget about forgetting. It is illusory.

Having forgotten about everything, including forgetting "forgetting," what cannot be forgotten stays.

With everything forgotten, your true nature as pure Consciousness stands revealed.

Be that.

I am

Disregard the collection of memories and thoughts that you usually associate with "I" or "me."

Focus on the primal "I am," on the "I," and let go of everything else. Feel your sense of being, your sense of existing. Abide there and allow everything to melt.

I exist

Do you exist? Recognize that you exist.

How do you know that you exist?

Abide in that knowingness. Abide in *That* which allows you to know that you exist.

Immersion

What is awareness? Is awareness male? Female? Does it have an age? Does it die? Was it born? Does it have any quality? Really answer these questions with a yes or no, through your own direct experience and knowingness.

Now, how did you know all that?

You knew it because you are that bodiless eternal attributeless awareness already. Immerse yourself in that recognition!

Let all come

Fear can come. Doubts can come. Sadness can come. Envy can come. Anger can come. Anxiety can come. Confusion can come. Frustration can come. Anything can come.

But, just as they come, they go. You stay as the unattached witness, merely "seeing."

When nothing seems to come anymore, abide in what is left, the empty primal awareness that you are.

Love

Feel love in your heart. Feel the love you have for God, for the inner Guru, or for your own consciousness.

Really allow love to sink into your heart, expanding toward your whole body and mind.

Now try to direct it at yourself, at your own consciousness. Intensely love your own consciousness. Intensely love the one who is loving. Merge the lover with the love.

Stay in that powerful love until there is no "I" to stay there.

Meditator

Rather than meditating on any perceivable object, meditate on the meditator. Meditate on the one who is meditating.

Your object of meditation is the meditator. Focus on that, concentrate on that, rest on that.

No Questions

Repose in the background that serves as the basis for all experiences.

If questions emerge, ignore them. Do not raise questions like, "Is this it? Is this awareness of no-thought, of empty spaciousness?" Such questions mean you are no longer abiding in empty awareness, in the substratum.

Alternatively, you can also follow the questions or experiences to their source, and they will dissolve in emptiness.

Nothing

Sit down and close your eyes. Do nothing.

Don't attempt to do anything.

Just let it be without trying to do nothing. Don't even try to "not do anything." Really do nothing, effortlessly.

Present

Recognize the present, the now.

Pay no attention to the past or to the future. Just the now.

Abide in this now-ness. Be present, be lucid, be aware. Be here. Be Conscious.

Recognize

Sit still, just witnessing the current content of your mind. When a thought comes, notice the source from where it came.

Just like you can easily smell an apple pie's fragrance when you're in your living room, which by following its aroma would lead you to the kitchen, you can "smell" back thoughts whence they came.

Follow a thought back to its source. Recognize that it came from nowhere, from an empty spacious awareness, it endured there, and subsided there.

Abide in that clear space of awareness, and even if thoughts come, let them come and disappear. You merely remain as the background space that allows them to appear and disappear.

Silence

Notice silence. Try to hear the silence. Close your eyes if you prefer. Really focus on hearing silence even if there's a lot of noise going on around you.

Once you can clearly hear silence, notice the one noticing the silence. Be aware of who is hearing the silence.

That's deeper than silence, that's before silence.

Dwell and marinate on *That*.

Silent Space of Being

Take a minute away from your thinking mind and recognize the clear space of awareness between thoughts.

What was aware of the thoughts?

That which is prior to thoughts. Live there.

Show no interest whatsoever in whatever your mind presents you with. Disregard all thoughts for a brief moment, and abide in that silent space of Being.

Be space. Be empty. Be nothing. Be.

Space

Notice space, merge with it. Become aware of empty space. Let your awareness expand toward space-awareness. Let your boundaries dissolve.

Now, who is aware of this all-pervading space? Is there an awareness of space, an awareness of being space, or an awareness of anything at all?

That awareness is where you have to be. It is bigger than the Universe, smaller than an atom, and bodiless at the same time.

Surrender

Why are you carrying weight that doesn't belong to you? Why are you identifying with thoughts that are not yours? Why are you believing that you are something that you are not?

Surrender all that weight. Surrender all those thoughts. Surrender all those beliefs. Surrender all those desires. Surrender your will. Surrender your story. Surrender your personality. Surrender your "I." Surrender the ego. Surrender everything that you can surrender. Surrender even the surrenderer.

Then let go. Let God fill you up. Be.

Time

Go back in time, billions of years, to the very beginning of the Universe. Go back to the singularity, to the beginning of time. Now go back even further, beyond time.

Or go further in time, trillions of years, to the very end of the Universe. Go to the end of time, to the singularity where everything will withdraw back into itself. Now go even further, beyond timc.

During deep dreamless sleep, you do not experience time. Time is non-existent there. Go back there, go back to no-time. Go beyond time.

What is the past but a thought? What is the future but a thought? When there are no thoughts, where is the past or the future? Where is time? Ponder deeply over these words.

You are beyond time. You arc awarc of timc when you're awake or dreaming, and aware of the absence of time when you're in deep sleep. You are before time, since it appears and disappears to you, the primordial empty awareness.

Un-enlightenment

Drop the concept of being "unenlightened." To think that you are not "enlightened" you have to go the mind and to the past. You have to go back with your mind and, based on your current evaluation of your experience, think "I am not enlightened."

Now, do not make any effort toward going either to the mind or to the past. Don't think about the past, don't try to conceive a future.

Without a past or a future, who are you? Presently, here and now, and not going to the past or to the future, who are you? In this exact instant, who is this past-less and future-less being?

In this instant, you are enlightened. Effortlessly, stay as you are. Don't become anything. Be Awareness.

Verbal-less

What does it mean to be aware? Don't answer verbally or with thoughts, but ponder this question deeply.

Be fully aware of how you answer this question by just being the answer.

Who or what is really aware? Be the answer.

Watcher

Watch whatever is in front of you. Really pay attention.

Now, watch the watcher. Watch the one who was watching seconds ago. You can close your eyes if you prefer, at this point.

Be still and just keep watching the watcher.

Who am I?

Ask yourself, "Who am I?" No verbal answer is needed, but just an awareness of the sense of being; an awareness of this "I" that you are. If needed, mentally say "I" and feel what this "I" is. Be aware of what is it like to be "I," or what being "I" feels like. Stay with "I" alone, until there is no more "I."

Witness

As you are reading the words in this book, these very words, notice that there is an awareness that is aware of the words being read. Yes, that very awareness, which is witnessing the reading of these words. Abide there. Witness the witnesser.

LOST IN THOUGHT AND MINI-DREAM IMAGERY

If you have lots of thoughts or mini-dream imagery popping up and preventing you from stably reposing in objectless awareness, this means that you still have work to do in the previous stage. Go back and do energetic practices like Kriya Yoga or Kundalini Yoga.

The purpose of all these mind-based practices is exactly that—stilling the mind so that it can repose on its source.

HALF-ASLEEP OR DULLNESS

If you are constantly falling asleep or feeling extremely dull and mentally lethargic, then, as mentioned above, you need to go back to doing the preliminary practices.

Post-practice awareness is an extraordinarily lucid and alert Self-Awareness state, rather than a dull half-asleep state. The kind of low-quality awareness that usually happens when we go to sleep and that leads only to dullness or drowsiness is the complete opposite of being consciously Present, or reposing in Awareness as explained in this book.

If sleepiness comes but you keep "doing" your best to "come back" to the background of consciousness as soon as you notice that your attention has been hijacked by some object, you will go past that half-asleep state. You will recognize this transition as a sudden "waking up" or a feeling of being "pulled up" into an extreme awareness of Being, as if you were suddenly extremely aware and awake, yet in profound silence and deep peace. Your body feels like a rock, and it could even be completely asleep, but your mind's alertness level will be through the roof. This can be called the mind-awake body-asleep state, akin to the sleep paralysis that occurs when we are sleeping, but with the particularity that we stay consciously aware.

When the gross senses are deactivated but you are still consciously lucid, real abidance in awareness can begin. With enough practice, you will go deeper and deeper, and a joy that you cannot contain will flourish up in your Heart. Following such bliss will take you even further into the depths of consciousness, beyond limits, beyond form, beyond duality.

PART III – BREAKING FREE

CHAPTER 17
WHAT ABOUT MY PERSONAL LIFE?

Whatever you do in your "personal life" should be an expression of the beauty of Being. For example, when the biggest artists this world has ever seen produced astonishing art, they did it from the depths of their being, from a state where the "I" had been shrunk to near nothingness, either knowingly, or in more likelihood, unknowingly. Commonly, they call it *inspiration*.

The ego can never create beautiful art. You will never do finer art than while being your true Self. The same happens in most other fields, whatever they might be, as long as they are somehow connected to your deepest inner calling.

See for yourself—remember that time you did something fantastic (not necessarily amazing to others, but to you, whatever that was)? How did you do it? Were you not in a state of natural and nearly effortless flow, a spontaneous dance with the present moment and totally absorbed in whatever you were doing? Space-time seems to fade away in those "diminished-ego" moments, as I've mentioned in the very first chapter of this book. Now, can you imagine the potential of your dual expression when there is no ego at all? It will be mind-blowing, in an unpretentious way. The finest dual expression is never an individual expression, but a cosmic expression, a universal, all-encompassing song, as if the Universe is singing through you.

Anyhow, you can be and do whatever you wish in life—but never forget about your true Being. Always remain consciously present, regardless of what you are doing. There are no problems in buying a new pair of shoes, a new smartphone, or any other things. But how do you feel about them? Do they bring you happiness? Do you feel better with them? There is no problem enjoying whatever the world brings, but if you are attached to those objects, then there is no doubt you will suffer. "Things," "money," "marriage," etc., are not the problem. The way you feel about them is. Will you feel terrible if you don't marry or if you can't buy that "new thing" you wish to buy? Please remember that it will all end, sooner or later. Nobody has promised you that your body will live until it is 90 years old. Even if it does, it will not last forever. It will pass away, just like all things in manifestation.

I don't mean that one should go live in a temple, an ashram or a cave. No, one doesn't have to be a monk. But it's your *earnestness, your deepest desire, your willingness to go all-in, even in the midst of whatever is happening in your life, that will dictate whether you make it now, or only in some future lifetime.*

To be brutally honest with you, I personally dropped every-thing. *Everything.* Only the truth mattered to me. It didn't matter if I died or stayed alive, if I lived in a house or on the streets, if I had money or no money. I didn't care. I promised myself I would do whatever it took to find God—to find myself. There was no life for me, except for the seeking of the Truth. Yes, it was quite drastic, but has anyone ever regretted being liberated? Buddha was asked about what he gained with meditation, with *nirvana.* He said he didn't gain anything but he lost a lot; he lost everything.

One will lose everything until what is left is what cannot be lost.

If you still have desires for the world and its promises, then perhaps you should go after them, while *always* continuing to do genuine sadhana "on the side," never forgetting about the search for the Truth. Keep the flame alive, burning, even if slightly dormant.

Eventually, there will come a time when your desires have been fulfilled, and you will see that you are still missing something; or your desires will never be fulfilled, and you will still miss something. Either way then, the level of commitment needed to go "all-in" into Self-discovery will wake up—unless one falls prey to another set of new desires that delusionally seem to fill that void.

CHAPTER **18**

THE WORLD IS YOURS

Since an early age, humans have been pursuing pleasure. It shapes and guides our lives. We want to avoid the bad and bathe in the good. This world is run by the search for pleasure, which is entirely different from the true inherent happiness of Being. It is but a distortion of that unbroken joy of the Self.

What then is the problem with the pursuit of pleasure?

It is pain.

Unfortunately, pleasure is always accompanied by pain, sorrow, unhappiness, fear, and so on.

Rather than seeking the Truth, most humans are wasting their lives in multiple ways, and only a few are genuinely turning away from the sources of their unhappiness.

Brief moments of happiness are what seem to make us tolerate this unhappiness, but can the craving for genuine happiness that people desire ever be found in the continuously changing objects of this world?

You already know the answer. Do not let the apparent pleasures of this world seduce you. Abide in the Presence of Being, and get to know real happiness, real joy, and real love.

By knowing the tremendous importance of being Present, rather than absent, highlighting the sense of aliveness within is of utter importance. Choose to be Present, even in the midst of demanding events, like the silent center of a tornado.

Life is not a tornado. However, the ego can create a tornado out of anything, especially since society seems to be guiding everyone in such direction, always telling us what to believe, what to think and how to act.

Society loves telling us what to do. Additionally, parents tell us what to do; teachers tell us what to do; bosses tell us what to do; traditions tell us what to do; gurus tell us what to do; everyone tells us what to do.

We've come a long way since the Stone Age, and now have incredibly advanced technology, but we still have made very little inward progress as a whole.

A long time ago, some rare beings were interested in investigating themselves, deep within. Today, some rare beings are interested in investigating themselves, deep within. It hasn't changed much; it's still way less than 0.1% of the world's population.

Society, which is the outward expression of humanity's current state of being, is far from being structured in such a way that encourages or teaches people to look at themselves, at their own self, to find peace and happiness. It will continue to stay like that unless humankind overcomes society's money-driven mentality. It is imperative to recognize that, regardless of what one thinks financial wealth can provide, it is nothing compared to the wealth of true bliss, peace, happiness, and completeness of recognizing our true deathless nature.

Freedom is not possible unless one realizes the ephemeralness of the world and how illusionary its appearance actually is. For such Insight to happen, one must be earnest and practice with true surrender and intention. Only then can true certainty about the unreality of the world arise.

It is imperative to let go of all *vasanas* and *samskaras*, all deep negative conditioning and subtle desires. The conditioning can be either pure or impure. The latter is what causes birth and death. The first is simply what sustains the body without any mental story or I-ness. It does not lead to any form of "reincarnation."

That is achieved through practice. Do not let your ego prevent you from actually putting in the time—it is really essential. If it weren't, all scholars and academics would be enlightened just by studying theory, reading scriptures or doing some incredible intellectual gymnastics. Even 5 to 10 minutes of practice per day make a tremendous difference.

Never forget that words come from the mind, hence they can never take us beyond their creator. Describing, explaining, demonstrating, storytelling, etc., are all great tools that work as *pointers*, but they can never walk us through the door of the Truth. They can show us the door, even open it, but only by being consciously Present, day after day, can we go through it.

Don't just read about enlightenment, really strive to make it your living reality! True contentment will then spontaneously shine in you, as you.

As long as you are not truly satisfied without having to do anything, you are still subject to sorrow, boredom, and dissatisfaction.

When you possess nothing, regardless of whether you live in the most majestic castle or in a forest, whether you travel by foot or by car, whether you have money or no money, whether you live alone or with a big family—all of which are irrelevant—then the world is truly yours. For you are unseparated from it.

Then the world can be said to be real, and no longer an illusion, because you, as Consciousness, are real. The world, as Consciousness is also real. What once was composed of name and form, being divided, is now "seen" as Consciousness itself, undivided and undifferentiated—One without a second.

> "The world is illusory;
> Brahman alone is real;
> Brahman is the world."
>
> - ADI SANKARA'S FAMOUS TEACHING

Just like gold exists without being made into an ornament, but a gold ornament can't exist without gold, so Consciousness exists without its own objects of consciousness, but obviously, they don't exist without it.

Consciousness is like gold, and even though a bracelet of gold is only gold, its characteristics and potential of creation are intrinsic and present in gold. In the same way, an object exists in the subject.

An object of consciousness exists in the consciousness that perceives it. But when consciousness abides in emptiness, without any objects, objects are removed. If you abide without objects long enough, then only the subject will remain. When only the subject remains, it is no longer a subject, since there are no objects to differentiate it. That which remains is the non-dual Ultimate Reality, where attribute-less pure Consciousness alone Is.

CHAPTER **19**

SURRENDERING

Surrendering is the greatest "action" the ego can perform. Not surrendering to someone, like a guru[25], but to the "highest"—your true Self, God. That's the key to Liberation, which will ultimately free you from ego-bondage.

Surrendering can never truly be conveyed by words because only each individual knows what they're holding on to that they don't want to let go of. Yet, *you undoubtedly know* that everything will have to go, eventually. So why are you trying to grab on to a shadow with a lock?

Resisting and not allowing whatever comes to come and whatever goes to go, makes the world seem much more real and enduring than it actually is, bringing much-unneeded

---

[25] Many people see a guru as the perfect embodiment of God, and worship him/her as if he/she were God. This is an error, for limiting the all-pervading Consciousness to a single body, is limiting the limitless. Surrendering to a *genuine* Guru is perfectly fine though, as long as one is not attached to his/her physical form, for the function of the outer Guru is only to take you to the inner Guru.

suffering. Life becomes a battle for survival, and your identity, your sense of separateness, which seems to be indispensable, becomes the biggest hurdle.

There is a high chance that during your spiritual journey, you will fear death at least once. It is a fact that the more you dispel the illusion that covers your true nature, the more your false identity, the false-self, becomes scared.

This can even be experienced as a near-death experience, just as many people have reported. It can happen out of the blue during the day, when you go to sleep, during the night, right when you wake up or as you do your spiritual practice (very rarely if ever during the techniques, but more-so during the after-practice state of Parvastha/Presence).

If you are progressing toward ego dissolution, then it is bound to happen at any time. It can also occur, extraordinarily, if you are suffering from a *massive* depression, but it is extremely unlikely, and depends on many conditions (a good deal of them not related to this current lifetime).

There should be no confusion though, since there is a big difference between the fear of death caused by spiritual practice—where your identity, bound to the body, is losing its usual body-awareness constraints and starts expanding toward a broader awareness—and the fear of death caused by any other reason. Yes, the fear of physical death is intimately connected to the fear of ego-dissolution, but moments before ego-dissolution, even if a tremendous fear of death appears out of nowhere, if one has been practicing correctly, deep down, there is a subtle *knowingness* regarding the fact that the dissolution of the ego is but a transient play of forms in the movie, rather than the immutable screen of consciousness.

It is at that precise moment, where the ego seems to face its end, that the biggest fear of your life will occur. It's the fear of facing nothingness, non-existence, death. It is here that surrender plays a big role. There's nothing you can do—it's out of your hands. Just a surrender beyond surrendering.

When one realizes that life is only a dream (all events, memories, desires, aspirations, problems, distresses, enjoyments, aversions, accomplishments, and so on) that appears, takes the spotlight, and fades into oblivion, the weight that one has been carrying the whole life just drops away.

Why are you carrying so much weight? Don't you recognize that you are on the train toward Freedom and that Life itself will take you to the destination? Why not enjoy the ride meanwhile, dropping your luggage on the floor and relaxing?

True surrender is knowing that, ultimately, despite what the ego might think, you are not in control. You've never really been in control, you just thought so. No person would intentionally choose to suffer, and if you are not always happy and at peace, are you really in control?

Realizing we are not in control, we can drop the luggage that had been causing us so much trouble, and align ourselves with the harmonious blissful universal vibration of Life. Life, filled with infinite intelligence, knows how to guide us better than we do, for Life itself is the dance of our absolute unmanifested Self.

CHAPTER **20**

YOU HAVE WHAT IT TAKES

There might be times, due to a powerful experience or Insight you've had, where you abide in such a blissful and peaceful state during your waking hours that there seems to be no end to it. You feel one with life, as if your own cells were made of happiness.

You are not thinking "I am enlightened," nor are you questioning "Am I not enlightened?". You simply and naturally live your life, permeated with an unbroken peace and joy. That peace-joy continues, whether walking, sitting, lying down, talking, being alone, in crowds, with family or friends, at work, and so on—it cannot be affected by daily life.

Yet, days or weeks later, either progressively or out of nowhere, you seem to have come back to your regular self. It is as if that peace-joy has evaporated. This can also happen when you visit an enlightened or advanced guru, where in his or her presence you feel entirely peaceful and complete, but then days after leaving that guru's physical presence, all seems to fade.

All of these moments, which are usually termed "enlightenment experiences," are not real enlightenment, but a prelude to it. Enlightenment cannot come and go.

See, who is it that had an "enlightenment experience"? Did the ego have it?

No, as you can clearly discern, the "egoic mind" eventually came back, "re-entering" your system—it wasn't present during the "enlightenment experience."

Therefore, who wants to recover or sustain the state of enlightenment for longer and longer? It is the ego, and it is giving you a very seductive and misleading thought (that you are identifying with), making you believe that you need to hold on to or regain the enlightenment state back. But see that the one who says or thinks "I need to hold on to that enlightenment state" or "I lost that state, and I must get it back" was not present during that enlightenment experience.

The "enlightenment state" did not suddenly appear when the egoic state of mind disappeared—it was already there and you just self-recognized it due to the temporary submerging of the ego-mind. It is ever-present, even with the superimposition of the egoic mind. Do not let the "ego's comebacks" create doubts or insecurity.

With enough practice, you become clear-headed and develop an enhanced awareness of whatever happens in your perceptive field, being more fully present, peaceful and joyful, and not getting caught up in the dramas created by the ego. However, there are still times when your previous tendencies, habits and unconscious ways of living flare up. Yes, it will happen—just don't make a big deal out of it. Be aware and keep staying as awareness, not re-identifying with the ego.

This is especially true when you come into contact with people who you have known for a long time, like your parents, relatives, old friends, old co-workers, etc.; when you visit certain places to which you have an emotional attachment (your parents' house, for example); or when certain stressful events occur. All these three scenarios can make you temporarily "asleep."

On the other hand, some individuals report the exact opposite, although it's rarer, mentioning that these "moments" make them more alert, aware, lucid and present.

Either way, you mustn't allow the ego, under any circumstances, to retake control of your life. Use the world as your playground, putting into practice your reaped insights and realizations.

One has to be ever-lucid because the ego—the false self—is always ready to use its tricks to push one back into the illusion of *Maya*. Doing sitting practices for a couple of hours per day, then giving the ego a blank check for the rest of the day, is neither the best nor the fastest way to find out our true infinite nature.

Yet, approaching the whole day with the burdensome task of always having to be alert to our current thoughts and ego-based patterns that prevent us from going beyond the mind, is not the way either.

Yes, constant vigilance and awareness are needed at first, but when it is put like that, it can seem like a chore, a task or a job to be aware, which will only lead to failure. That's because the "you" who is "practicing" being aware the whole day, is not able to do it.

Let's try to understand this point:

When your body was born, it didn't come with your name on it. No body comes with a name. Someone, perhaps your parents, decided to name that body. Let's suppose they called you "Alex."

When they gave you that name, you were unaware of it—it meant nothing to you! It was just another sound people around you uttered. With time, as you grew up, that name started to become imprinted in your consciousness. The consciousness could then "hold" the impression of the name "Alex," adopting it and referring it to itself: "I am Alex." When someone asked you who you are, that's what you would answer. Before that, you were nameless. Furthermore, this association was hugely reinforced by society, friends, parents and so on. When looking at a picture, your parents or friends pointed to your body and said, "There you are."

However, that name is not original to you. It came, and you embedded it in yourself. After being naturally interiorized, you didn't have to remember it consciously. Whenever someone called you ("Hey, Alex!"), you would instantly respond, without needing to actively remember your name over and over again.

The same happens with gender. You don't have to constantly remember that you have a male or female body. Once it gets truly interiorized, you simply know, all the time, without having to keep forcing or remembering it over and over again.

You don't have to actively remember who you are (Consciousness). Actually, you're not actively remembering or forgetting your true Self. It's only because of the identification with the ego-mind that you can say "I stay as awareness, then I lose my attention and the ego returns."

The truth is that *even before remembering and forgetting came*, you are pure Consciousness already. I know this might be hard for the mind to understand, but a seed is being planted deep down in your being, which will sprout into a beautiful flower. Something in you knows this to be true and will start coming up to the surface. Let *That* which this book points toward reveal itself to you, settling in your consciousness, becoming your true and direct experience.

You already have this power in you—you just forgot it was there and now you look to the mind for help, like you are used to doing. It is the ego-mind that plants the seed of doubt, the seed of forgetfulness.

It's best that you look at your Heart, at your own consciousness, since when it comes to finding out who we truly are, we have to go beyond the mind—and there—the mind can't help us.

The whole spiritual process is not about learning new things, but more about letting go—letting go of all the illusions, letting go of the ego.

Never again will you be living in a human's habitual routine of fear and dissatisfaction. When the body-mind is no longer your home, you are no longer bound by time and space. You are centerless, and everywhere is your center.

CHAPTER **21**

NOTHING

In a remote village, there was an old enlightened Master who lived a humble and simple life. His only possessions were the ragged clothes he always wore, and a walking stick that had been passed down from Master to disciple through ten generations. His Master had given him the walking stick 30 years previously, just before passing away. This walking stick was made of wood with a big shiny diamond on the top front.

Rumors from the neighboring villages were that this diamond was magical and therefore extremely valuable. However, no one had ever attempted to steal it, for it belonged to a supremely wise, kind and loving man who was always willing to help anyone at any time. He guided the modest people of his village, and others who came from other villages, one step at a time, toward their inner realms, to find true happiness within. Most of the people in his village were his disciples, and they frequently came to him for advice. His fame quickly spread throughout the entire country.

News of the wisdom and kindness of the old enlightened Master made it to the ears of the King, who was the supreme ruler of the country. The King hated that someone was becoming popular amongst the population, and feared that his reign as the commander-in-chief might soon be challenged.

Thus, he decided to elaborate a plan. He secretly called his most trusted guard and said:

"I will inform the leader of each village that one week from today, a big ceremony will be held in the village where the supposedly enlightened old man lives, to honor him. Everyone will be present. Then, three days from now, I shall leave this city and go to that village. Upon arriving, I will pretend to be a poor farmer looking for guidance, and I will offer my services to the old man. I will put on an act and become his disciple."

"Okay, my King. And what shall I do?" asked the guard.

"You will leave the castle the day after I leave, and you shall go to the same village. On the day of the ceremony, I, as a fake disciple, will ask the old man to speak to the crowd. As soon as he starts speaking, you go up and hit him on the leg and then steal his walking stick. Then you shall break that stick, remove the diamond, and run, right in front of everyone." The King said, maliciously. "Do not worry, as you will be highly rewarded for this mission."

The guard nodded and was ready to leave the King's room when he heard the King speak aloud: "Then, everyone will see how unenlightened that old man is! I can't wait to see his face as I take away his precious 400-hundred-year-old stick and diamond! I will then regain first place in people's minds as the most popular, wise and powerful person in the country!"

One week later, the big day came. Every village's leader had gathered in that remote village, and the King had successfully pretended to be a poor farmer. He had been sleeping in the old Master's house, and had been given food and kindness, but decided to proceed with the plan anyway. He was blinded by his own fears and insecurities.

When every villager and leader were gathered in the center of the village, the King told the Master that he should speak some wise words, because after all, everyone was there for him. The Master agreed and went up on the stage that had been temporarily set up for the occasion, with the help of his walking stick.

As he was about to speak, a hooded man came running up onto the stage and hit him on the leg, making him fall, stealing his stick, breaking it and removing the diamond, and then escaping right afterward.

The Master simply got up, with a bit of effort, and smiled as if nothing had happened, not even looking in the direction of the robber.

Everyone was in shock and started screaming "Who was that man?! What just happened? How come he hit you, stole your walking stick and diamond, ran away, and you are still there smiling and doing nothing?"

Laughing, the Master said:

"Nothing happened to me. Before this body was born, I was nothing. When this body was born, I was nothing. When I had the body of a child, I was nothing. When the body became an adult body, I was nothing. Now, with an old body, I still am nothing. After I drop this body, I will still be nothing. If I am already nothing, how can I lose something? How can nothing be hurt? Who can steal from nothing? Who can touch nothing?

With or without the walking stick and the diamond, I am still the same. With or without the body, I am still the same. With or without 'I,' I am still the same. Even when I'm not the same, I'm still the same. Who can comprehend such truths? Only those who are nothing. *Only nothing can comprehend no-thingness.*"

The King was in awe. He instantly revealed his true personal identity and came to the stage to bow to the Master. He was utterly sorry and started crying.

The Master, with his infinite compassion and uncompromising clarity, turned to the King and, grabbing his hand, said:

"Get up my son. You are neither a poor farmer nor a rich King. You and I are the same, and have always been. Just as you dropped your false farmer identity, drop your royal disguise too.

Be what you already are. Don't be afraid to be nothing. To be the whole, you have to become nothing."

CHAPTER **22**

THE HEART OF CONSCIOUSNESS

When you reach a certain stage, you will not ask for anything. There is no one to ask and nothing to be asked for. Whatever comes, comes. Whatever goes, goes. Everything flows naturally, without wishes or intentions. This is not an individual, egoic accomplishment. It is as if life is not being lived by an individual anymore, but by the whole Universe. It unfolds spontaneously like a flower blooming in the spring.

Being enlightened is not a mental or intellectual knowingness. All the knowledge you have accumulated in your mind since you were young, primarily based on your sense of identity has to go.

Everything has to be erased. The ego is not your identity. Your idea of who you are is not your identity. Your self-image is not your identity. Objectless and boundless Consciousness is your identity, or if you prefer, you can say you are really identity-less!

Now, this doesn't mean that if you go to the doctor and the doctor calls you by your name and points at your body, that you're going to answer "I'm boundless consciousness, not this name and body, doctor!" No, one could say one is like an actor, playing the game of this motion picture, never identified with it and always remaining as the subject.

What's even the problem of using the word "I"? Uttering "I" or "mine" has neither meaning nor weight to the one who is Free. That merely happens from the perspective of the observer, mistaking the enlightened being's body and mind to be someone, some person. As long as one is not Free, one will not truly understand these words.

Identification is only a phenomenon; it's an ever-changing self-portrait. Why cling to something that will never be more than a work in progress? You are the substratum in which everything happens, even the identification. A pure stainless canvas, painted with the love of duality, yet untainted.

Even what once was believed to be true, the "need for Liberation," due to the ego, is found to be an illusion. The ego-ghost, despite all of its tricks, stratagems, schemes, strategies, and deceptions, is found to be non-existent. Searching for a ghost reveals the Light.

Something that has caused you so much trouble and so much suffering, is in the end, non-existent. This might come as a shock, but you don't need to believe it. You need to realize it.

The snake is not really a snake, but a rope! The darkness of ignorance caused us to see the rope as a snake, but now, with the clear light of Being, we see a rope for what it is—a rope. Never has the rope been a snake, but it was believed so! So is the ego.

This Truth is not hard to realize. Unlearning everything you have learned, abiding in your own sense of Being, Love will rise up. Love is the most powerful force in the Universe. Love is not a physical or an emotional attraction. It is not a feeling.

Love is indescribable, and can only truly be experienced when there is no more "you" or "me." This Oneness, this interconnectedness, this union, this infinite wholeness, is the most joyful roar of Freedom.

Our love for anything in the world is only for its true essence, which is our true common essence. We don't love objects—we love the Self alone. Not "we" as an ego-mind, but "we" as awareness, and definitely not a self as an "ego-self" but a Selfless Self—impersonal Being-Consciousness-Bliss. It *is*, and it is *aware* of itself, as itself only—and that is infinitely *blissful*. It is completeness without limitation, incomprehensible to the human mind.

Awareness being only aware of itself is true non-duality. No one can deny Awareness, for its very denial is an acknowledgment of Awareness. Even if there were a recognition of non-existence, non-awareness or non-being, there would have to be Awareness. Awareness indisputably serves as the basis even for "non-awareness." This is not a conclusion based on inference—it can be directly realized. It is not true for the mind, but it is true for the real you, pure Awareness.

The "state" of uninterrupted Self-Awareness is truly the mark of an enlightened being—it is called Sahaja Samadhi, the natural state.

It is not achievable by any human being because a human can never really be enlightened. It is God that is ever-enlightened, and putting a veil over "Himself," believes "Himself" to be a limited consciousness in a body. Breaking free from that self-imposed veil, God rediscovers God. It is always God that rediscovers God—only the infinite can realize its infiniteness. All, while staying ever veil-less and the same.

Do you realize the implication of such words? *You are God already*. Wake up!

"All things arise, suffer change, and pass away.
This is their nature.

When you know this, nothing perturbs you, nothing hurts you.
You become still. It is easy.

God made all things. There is only God.
When you know this, desire melts away.

Clinging to nothing, you become still."

"You are pure. You are still.

The world with all its wonders
Is nothing.

When you know this, desire melts away.
For you are Awareness itself.

When you know in your heart that there is nothing,
You are still."

— ASHTAVAKRA GITA

For ages you have been trapped inside the cage of your own mind. An imagined cage which was believed so strongly that you felt it was as real as reality itself.

But your eyes have been opened. You cannot unsee what has been seen.

And what has been seen?

You.

You have seen yourself.

Tears of joy come out of your Heart, for the pure love for yourself is unfathomable. You are the whole creation and beyond. Each tear is a Universe.

So it continues, with every breath and tear of joy, directly from the Heart of God—the Heart of Consciousness.

If you enjoyed reading this book and it helped you see what you hadn't seen before, especially regarding the ego and the Truth, **please show your support by leaving a *Review on the Amazon page.***

It really makes a difference.
It helps to spread the true teachings to those who are genuinely seeking them.

Thank you.

Subscribe and receive the ebook **Uncovering the Real** plus updates and information regarding new books or articles, which will be sent about once a month.

www.RealYoga.info

If you have any doubts or questions regarding this or any of the other books, feel free to contact me at:

Santata@RealYoga.info

Read also, by the same author of *The Yoga of Consciousness*:

— KRIYA YOGA EXPOSED

The Truth About Current Kriya Yoga Gurus & Organizations.
Going Beyond Kriya, Contains the Explanation of a Special Technique
Never Revealed Before In Kriya Literature.

— THE SECRET POWER OF KRIYA YOGA

Revealing the Fastest Path to Enlightenment.
How Fusing Bhakti & Jnana Yoga into Kriya will Unleash the most
Powerful Yoga Ever.

— KUNDALINI EXPOSED

Disclosing the Cosmic Mystery of Kundalini.
The Ultimate Guide to Kundalini Yoga, Kundalini Awakening,
Rising, and Reposing on its Hidden Throne.

Available @ Amazon as Kindle & Paperback.

GLOSSARY

Advaita - Non-duality.

Anapanasati - Buddhist practice of mindfulness of breathing.

Awakening - There are different levels of awakening, which go from minor Insights and realizations, to the final "awakening" or final "Insight" which is regarding one's true deathless and bodiless nature (Enlightenment).

Brahman - The Ultimate Reality, the Absolute. Some call it **Para-brahman** or **Nirguna Brahman**, which means Highest Brahman or Brahman without form or qualities.

God - Although I have written God as "Himself," God is neither male nor female.

Kabbalah - Esoteric spiritual discipline originated in Judaism.

Kriya Supreme Fire - Method to awake the Kundalini, as explained in Kriya Yoga Exposed and Kundalini Exposed.

Kundalini - Primal spiritual energy said to be located at the base of the spine. For a deeper understanding, read *Kundalini Exposed*.

Maya - The veil of illusion that covers our true infinite nature.

Parvastha - The "After-Kriya" blissful Self-Awareness state.

Prana - Life Force.

Pranayama - Life-force restraint/control technique.

Rajasic Guna - the quality of passion, activity, motion, excitement, self-centeredness, etc.

Sadhana - Spiritual Practice.

Samadhi - Absorption, higher state of consciousness.

Samatha - Buddhist name for one-pointed meditation that culminates in effortless, joyful attention.

Satguru - the true Guru; the inner Guru; God within.

Satsang - Association with being, or, alternatively, being in the presence of a Self-Realized Master.

Sattvic Guna - the quality of compassion, balance, equilibrium, peace, purity, etc.

Self - With a capital "S" means pure Consciousness or pure Awareness, devoid of any objects. Unless specified otherwise, in this book, awareness and consciousness are used interchangeably; self with a small "s" is synonymous with ego or "I."

Shakti - Personification of Kundalini, the life-force principle that gives life the Universe.

Sleep Paralysis – Mind awake, body asleep phenomenon. It is when, during awakening or falling asleep, a person is aware but unable to move, speak or control the breath.

Spiritual Heart - The rarely mentioned Causal Center. Refer to Kundalini Exposed, chapter 12 for more information.

Sushumna Nadi - The subtle channel through which the life-force flows, located in the middle of the spine.

Tamasic Guna - the quality of ignorance, impurity, dullness, inertia, etc.

The Secret / The Law of Attraction - a best-selling self-help book based on the law of attraction which claims that thoughts can change the world directly.

Vasanas / Samskaras - Latent tendencies stored in the causal body, responsible for reincarnation.

Vipassana - Buddhist name for self-introspection through abiding in awareness which will culminate in Insight into the nature of reality.

Printed in Great Britain
by Amazon